Real kids
in an **Unreal** world

Building Resilience and Self Esteem in Todays Children

Pennington Publications

PO Box 312 Murwillumbah, NSW 2484
Website: www.maggiedent.com

First Published September 2008

Title: Real Kids in an Unreal World: Building Resilience and Self Esteem in Today's Children
Edition: First
Author: Dent, Maggie

Date of Publication: 11th September 2008

ISBN: 978-0-9758456-1-5

1. healthy parenting, 2. building resilience and coping skills 3. good nutrition
4. importance of boundaries 5. value of children's play 6. self esteem
7. practical parenting tips and strategies 8. strengthening children's spirits
9. community importance 10. preventative focus in childhood

Layout and Design: Katharine Middleton

"To the world you may be just one person, but to one person you may be the world."

Josephine Billings

Dedication

This book is dedicated to three very special
women who became a really important part of my sons' lives.
These caregivers loved and cared for my precious sons in our
home from time to time while they were children. Each
beautiful soul became a part of our family and a special part
of the happy memories we all have of those magical, chaotic
years.

Thank you so much

Kate Leigh (dec) – "Our Kate",

Jenny O'Halloran née Trigwell

Chrissy Paisley

Contents

Acknowledgements

My first thank you goes to the Western Australian government Department for Communities for giving me the privilege of running the Enriching Resilience in Children initiative in 2007.

I offer my deepest thank you to the following special people in my humble life:

To my wonderful P.A. or my admin angel from heaven Liz Guidera, thank you for managing my diary and for supporting my passion to help families in the healthy raising of children.

To my graphic angel and special friend Katharine Middleton who has been my typesetter and graphic designer—thank you again for another book birthed safely.

To my editors and proofreaders Janney Wale and Tiffany Garvie who tame my text and correct my syntax with such skill.

To my national book distributor Peter De Cort from Australian Book Group—thank you for your continued support and advice.

To my supportive and patient husband Steve who has been there every step on this journey. Thank you for the cups of tea and the shoulder rubs.

To my amazing four sons Michael, Ben, Alex and James - who have been both wonderful teachers and students in my life journey and who continually make me feel blessed.

To my four-legged secretary and support Jess who sat at my feet keeping me company, yet again, whenever I was in my office writing.

Maggie

Once Upon a Time

Homo erectus, an early form of human, existed between 1.8 million and 300,000 years ago. This human walked upright and used fire and rudimentary tools. The species existed in Africa, Asia and Europe.

From these early beginnings humans have evolved and made changes in response to the environment in which he and she lives. For homo erectus to survive and conquer the environment, the species had to learn how to live in communities and successfully raise children.

Homo sapiens, or modern humans, appeared 195,000 years ago. This human lived in tribal communities all around the globe. Communities needed the cooperation of everyone to survive from day to day. There were clear divisions of labour for men and women. Very specific social and cultural patterns of interaction were also played out in these very early communities. Everyone was committed to working toward the greater good of the tribe in order to maximise survival.

Indigenous tribes around the world continued living this way. Communities in parts of Europe continued developing, and after the Middle Ages they eventually adopted what has become the Western way of living. The Australian Aborigines lived in the same types of communities for over 50,000 years before the arrival of white settlers. They took care of their country, their culture and their tribes, both holistically and respectfully.

The tribal approach to living was communal. Children were raised as part of the community, which meant that everyone shared in the healthy raising of children. The elderly were revered as the keepers of lore and wisdom, and were a valued part of their tribe. Teenagers were prepared for adulthood, and initiation and ceremony were markers for the beginning of a new stage of life. Communities worked together to feed and protect each other. Members came together to eat, dance, create and share resources. This tribal approach defines the expression:

It takes a whole village
to raise a child.

Introduction

Our modern world is so full of innovations, new knowledge and ways of doing things that we should all be in great shape. Unfortunately, we are not. Many parents and teachers are deeply concerned about our children and teenagers, and how they are struggling to manage or cope with the pressures of modern living. We have reached a new level of concern. Both research and statistics support the perception of declining health and well being for our young. Of most concern is the increasing numbers of children and teenagers who are succumbing to depression, emotional instability, mental illnesses, obesity and low educational and social competence. Today's families and communities are struggling.

This book explores how parents can ensure that their children grow healthy, with skills that help them manage living in our modern world and encourage them to become worthwhile adults. The ability to cope with and conquer all that life brings is built in the early years between 0–12 years of age. This book offers ideas about how to build resilience and a positive sense of self in our children. Our modern lifestyle has destroyed the 'whole village' pattern of raising children. Parents now have sole responsibility for raising their children rather than it being a collective responsibility. We are paying a big price for this individualistic approach to parenting.

Much of the damage done to young children is avoidable or preventable, however let's not disappear down Alice's rabbit hole. There never has been a perfect way of raising children, even in a tribal context. Childhood is a journey and there is no perfect world, parent or way to raise a child. Remember, there is no perfect child. Families today live in a world of massive change and uncertainty. The reality is that parenting is now harder than it has ever been before. However, real kids can thrive in our unreal world.

Many of the pressures and challenges on families today are invisible. What is helpful on one level can be destructive on another, such as TVs, mobile phones, the Internet and MP3 players. Being affluent and having the ability to give your children the things you were unable to have as a child should be a good thing. Unfortunately, affluence can create challenges to raising resilient children, more so than financial challenges or adversity.

The very experience of having to save for something, or wait for it, makes the receiving of what is desired so much sweeter. Being able to delay gratification is seen as a key quality for an emotionally mature person. The 'Y generation' has immediate access to plastic credit and the temptations it brings before they have the maturity to manage the full consequences of their actions.

> 80% of your chances of being successful in life have to do with your emotional intelligence rather than your cognitive intelligence.
>
> *Emotional Intelligence,*, Daniel Goleman (1995).

We know more than ever about how the human brain develops as a child grows. This has massive implications for parents and parenting.

Do any of the following challenging questions interest you?

- How do you build the coping skills in your children so that as adults, they successfully manage the continuous change occurring in their world?
- What are some of the most important life skills to teach your child?
- How do you best support a child to grow into who they are 'meant to be', not who you think they 'should be'?
- What attributes provide your child with mental and emotional well-being?
- How do you build character and social competence in your child?
- How can parents be mindful of ways to prevent their child attempting suicide—at any age?

- What things can you do as a parent to build your child's capacity to manage and cope, while still allowing the child to have a childhood that is safe and life enhancing?
- What things are really important to include in your child's life that supports them to grow into a person who makes the world a better place?
- What will help your child be a friendly, cooperative and caring person?
- What can you do to ensure that your child realises his or her full potential in life?
- How do you ensure that your child develops positive values and a healthy sense of self?
- How can you enjoy your parenting journey more?
- How do you do all of the above at the same time as running flat out on the treadmill of work and raising children?

> The strongest oak of the forest is not the one that is protected from the storm and hidden from the sun. It's the one that stands in the open where it is compelled to struggle for its existence against the winds and rains and the scorching sun.
>
> Napoleon Hill (1883-1970).

Background

What is resilience?

Resilience refers to the ability to successfully manage your life and adapt to change and stressful events in healthy and constructive ways. In simple terms, it is our survivability and ability to 'bounce back' from life's experiences; both those that are advantageous and the really challenging, traumatic ones. Two other helpful definitions of resilience are:

> *"An individual's ability to thrive and fulfil potential despite or perhaps because of stressors or risk factors."*
>
> *James Neill.*

> *A universal capacity which allows a person, group or community to prevent, minimize or overcome the damaging effects of adversity.*
>
> *The International Resilience Project, (2005).*

The importance of resilience in today's world

Young people have always needed effective coping skills, however the modern world is more challenging than ever before. It appears that many of our young people have fewer resources to be able to deal with adversity than in previous generations. Our main concerns today involve the increasing numbers of young people who are aggressive, depressed and suicidal, and engage in maladaptive coping strategies such as substance abuse and antisocial behaviour. Sleep disorders and anxiety problems are also increasingly real concerns for those who work with troubled, unwell children – some as young as two or three years old.

It is essential for parents and carers of children to improve their understanding of resilience. An understanding offers insights into how we can protect our children from the damaging effects of the pressures in our increasingly chaotic and uncertain world, *without over protecting them.*

Today's world is very different from that in which many parents were raised. The enormous information explosion, technological advances, consumerism and rapid pace of life seems to have created a unique disease called 'modernism'. The expectation that our youth should be smarter and healthier is not always true. Experts working in research and health sciences are identifying more teenage pregnancies, depression, anxiety disorders, violence, and illicit and social drug use. There is more family disharmony and homelessness; literacy rates and school successes are also reduced.

The most tragic example of low resilience is suicide, when an individual chooses to end his or her life because living has become too hard. That is why it is important to raise awareness in communities and homes about how we can build and enrich resilience in today's children and teenagers. Overwhelmingly, research reinforces how crucial the early years are in developing life-long resilience.

Building resilience is a vital ingredient in our parenting. It is a process that directs our interactions with our children as we strengthen their ability to meet life's challenges and pressures with confidence and perseverance.

> Thirty years of research tells us that resilient people are happier, live longer and are more successful in school and jobs, are happier in relationships and are less likely to suffer depression.
>
> K. Reivich and A. Shatte (2002);
> *Journeys from Childhood to Midlife: Risk, Resilience, and Recovery*, E. Werner and R. Smith (2001).

Bonnie Benard is considered by many as the mother of the concept of building resilience. She worked for many years with children who were at risk. Bonnie decided that, rather than focusing on what was wrong in these children's lives, she would explore what was working. What was helping them to cope with their very dysfunctional lives? With her innovative vision she identified protective factors. Communities could develop these factors to build resilience, especially in young people. The 10 Building Blocks model that is explored in this book as a way of building resilience in children is based on Bonnie Benard's focus on protective factors. This focus allows us to focus on the strengths in a child's life rather than focusing on what's wrong. In many ways we now "over-pathologise" children in today's world.

> *"The number of psychiatric diagnoses for childhood conditions has soared in the last two decades, increasing from about 70 conditions to more than 400. What this means is that "what was once considered within the bounds of normal is now treated as an illness requiring a cure, which more often than not comes in the form of medication".*
>
> Dr George Halasz a Melbourne psychiatrist

Not only do we tend to focus on what's wrong with our children or what's delayed in their development, we are busy hurrying them up. This model supports the "slow childhood down" movement that allows real kids time to be kids, instead of being hot housed and pushed into early adolescence before they have been able to be healthy kids. It takes lots of time, energy and loving care to raise healthy children, and with awareness it is still very possible in today's unreal world. It all starts in the first 5 years.

The essential early years

The early years right from conception are vital periods in which we can help our children to be better equipped to live in this chaotic world of continual, rapid change. Key building blocks can strengthen our ability to be resilient and bounce back from the bumps and bruises of life. These building blocks can create vital, protective factors that strengthen our capacity to cope and overcome adversity. The first five years of a child's life will lay down the foundations for their future mental, emotional, social and psychological health. We must invest more heavily than ever before in these early years to support families. This model is aimed at doing just that by using common sense and the latest child development research from around the world.

During the early years of a child's life, it is not only physical and intellectual development that is occurring rapidly, emotional and social development is also quickly developing. Most of the important developments are imperceptible and are difficult to measure as they happen. Often the little things are the big things.

Today's parents have many pressures and choices to make and are exposed to many conflicting theories about what is best for their children. Just take a look in any good book store at the range of parenting books, manuals and glossy magazines. Have you noticed how well groomed and fresh faced the parents appear in these parenting magazines? I am yet to see a picture of a parent showing obvious signs of sleep deprivation, carrying excess weight or having a frustrating parenting moment. Then there are the celebrity parenting experts. They are giving advice about parenting and their children are still under 10 years of age. Sorry, but you cannot give any serious advice to the global audience until you have children over 23 years of age, when you can fully see the effects of your parenting in the early years.

TV shows take parenting expertise into homes everywhere. It is no wonder we have the notion that parenting is a type of competition. This is apparent with parents spending a lot of money on accelerated learning classes for children as young as four years of age; but there is no such thing as a perfect parent or child. Perfection is a very unhuman thing and those people who have tendencies toward perfection will share this fact with you.
Developmental aspects which impede mastery in some areas of a child's development can show up at any time in their life. Today's world is in a big hurry. It pressures children, or their parents, to meet deadlines and learning targets—often before they are ready. Early failures can shape a child's belief in themselves and change their belief system for life, which may cause other psychological challenges later in life.

We all have moments when we show excellence, and other moments when we are far from excellent. That is the nature of life. We all worry about how our children are going to turn out— and there are lots of children who worry about how their parents are going to turn out! The finishing line is the moment when we exhale the last breath from our body, and until that moment, we are still working on making our way through the journey of life. Actually living and embracing all that life delivers, instead of worrying about what could and might happen, would help many people to enjoy it more. Parenting is a bit like that too.

What was insightful and wonderful for me about researching the model of 10 Building Blocks was gaining an awareness that raising healthy, happy children has not really changed, despite the evolving world. You don't need a lot of money to raise children well, you just need to provide these basics:

- Plenty of loving interaction with significant people who care for them.
- Interesting environments to explore.
- Enormous amounts of play.
- Opportunities to make mistakes and learn from them.

> What a child really needs is good, positive emotional relationships with parents and others. They don't need a thousand activities. Children can learn facts and gain external skills at any time. But they only gain relationship skills when young.
>
> *Parents' Magazine*, Ruth Schmidt Neven, Director of the Centre for Child and Family Development, Melbourne, November (2004).

Fortunately, with the advance of the neurosciences, brain research and other technology, we are now better able to understand what helps create better resilience in all of us. There are key building blocks that strengthen our ability to be resilient, and the more building blocks present in a child's life, the more protective factors will be present later in life. Many of these qualities are hard to measure and quantify, and this makes it difficult for some parents to know just how their child is developing – these building blocks give a universal language that can help parents to know what will matter later in life.

Characteristics of resilient people

- *An ability to bounce back and recover from almost anything.*

- *Optimistic and flexible thinking skills.*

- *A 'where there's a will there's a way' attitude.*

- *Seeing problems as opportunities to learn and grow.*

- *An ability to persevere and persist.*

- *A healthy and authentic self esteem.*

- *A capability to set clear, realistic and attainable goals.*

- *Having a healthy social support network.*

- *Seldom dwelling on the past or the future.*

- *Well developed emotional and spiritual competence.*

- *An ability to learn from previous challenges and mistakes.*

- *A capacity for detachment.*

- *A well developed sense of humour.*

- *The ability to have meaningful involvement with other individuals and their communities.*

- *Treat themselves and others with respect.*

- *Good problem solving and conflict resolution skills.*

10 Resilience Building Blocks for Children 0–12 years of age

1. Positive healthy pregnancy.
2. Good nutrition.
3. Safe, nurturing care within the circle of family.
4. Plenty of play.
5. Building life skills.
6. Meaningful Involvement with positive adults.
7. Clear boundaries.
8. Absence of stress.
9. Self mastery.
10. Strengthening the spirit.

This model outlines 10 essential building blocks for 0–12 year olds that build healthy self esteem and strengthen a child's ability to be resilient and bounce back from life's challenges. These building blocks highlight the different areas that a parent, school or community can focus on in order to build resilience for life. Any of the building blocks will help, and the more you nurture the better. The only block that can be used only once is obviously the first—Positive, healthy pregnancy. I have never met a woman who wants to repeat any pregnancy!

10 Resilience Building Blocks

for children aged 0 - 12 years

10

Strengthen the spirit

8

Absence of stress

9

Self mastery

5

Build life skills

6

Meaningful involvement
with positive adults

7

Clear boundaries

1

Positive healthy
pregnancy

2

Good nutrition

3

Safe nurturing care within
the circle of family

4

Plenty of play

In the tribal context, women's business was taken very seriously. Each woman was supported by other women, especially when they were expecting or had a new baby. They were given food, care and respect because they were bringing a miracle into the tribe, a new life. This was something that was deeply respected and honoured, and seen as a sacred privilege.

Building Block 1
Positive, healthy pregnancy

The first step in building healthy, resilient children is for mothers to have stress free pregnancies in which they have loving support, excellent nutrition and an absence of alcohol or medically unauthorised drugs.

It was previously considered that babies arrived with a clean slate; that everything they learned took place after birth. Research now shows that a foetus is responsive to its mother's changing emotional state, which is passed hormonally across the placenta. Stressful and traumatic experiences that a mother has while the infant is in the womb, and throughout the early months of life, are registered in a child's brain as 'emotional memory'. They help to shape both the forming psyche and the personality of a child.

> Behavioural disturbances as serious as delinquency, schizophrenia, ADHD, depression and substance abuse have been associated with highly stressful experiences in the womb; such as severe marital discord, or maternal hostility or rejection towards the foetus.
>
> *Parenting for a Peaceful World: Robin Grille* (2006)

Avoiding alcohol, especially in the first three months (the first trimester) of pregnancy, assists the development of a healthy brain. Research proves how alcohol abuse damages a baby's brain and impedes early development on all levels. This creates a challenge for developing life resilience. In the United States of America, the number one cause of mental retardation is maternal alcohol abuse—which is 100% preventable. Serious alcohol abuse can result in the baby being born with FADS (foetal alcohol spectrum disorders), which creates mental, social and emotional problems in the baby for life.

A mother experiencing physical and emotional abuse causes stress for both mother and baby. We can help those we love by creating support networks and providing caring respite. Family and friends of a pregnant mother need to be present during the pregnancy to support the mother as much as possible. Healthy food, exercise and supplementation—especially of folic acid and iron—provide the expectant mother with the best chance of delivering a healthy baby. Some foods are not recommended during pregnancy and it is up to the doctor attending the expectant mother to provide her with this information. Smoking is one of the things to avoid, both during pregnancy and when around children. Genetic defects, abuse of any kind, brain insults and bad environments immediately after birth (post partum) can contribute to an unhealthy brain and poor baby development.

In many cultures today it is still common to see the whole family taking responsibility for raising a child and assisting the mother. This includes help from older siblings, extended family and other community members. Aboriginal and New Guinean tribal cultures; and Asian and African cultures are examples. In these cultures, caring for mothers-to-be can include:
- natural birthing practices that protect vital mother/baby bonding
- breast feeding—often for two years and beyond
- babies spending the majority of time in human contact, being carried in the arms or in slings
- babies and children being cared for by grandparents and relatives.

These traditional cultures are considered to be high touch. This creates a positive environment for babies to be nurtured. Meredith F. Small PhD wrote the book *Our Babies, Ourselves:*

How Biology and Culture Shape the Way we Parent. She reported a survey of 186 societies in which researchers found that infants were carried most of the time in non-industrial societies, 56% of the time in traditional societies, and only 25% of the time in the USA.

> Many of the infant and child behaviours that are challenging parents in our culture are unheard of in cultures that practise high-touch nurturing. Babies are biologically programmed to expect the same high-touch nurturing that evolved millions of years ago.
>
> *Connection Parenting*, Pam Leo in *Kindred Magazine* (June-August 2008).

In our modern world there is a need to build supportive networks for mothers-to-be. Non-biological friendship groups that act as extended families work very well. It also helps if an expectant mother can develop a relationship with community services like play groups, family centres and neighbourhood groups. Social isolation can be dangerous mentally and emotionally when new babies are around. Sleep deprivation is unpleasant for everyone – offering respite to a new Mum is helpful for mum and baby. We all need to offer more support before and after the arrival of a new baby.
An excellent resource for first time mothers that has been written by a very wise 84 year old mid wife who spent most of her life helping new Mums is called "No One Right Way" by Rhodanthe Lipsett. It covers everything – absolutely everything a new Mum may need to know in the first 3 months of a new baby's life.

One of my sons asked me what was happening with my bottom while I was pregnant with his brother. I told him I had a baby growing in my tummy. He said he knew that, but what was growing in my bum?

> When babies are born to mothers who have taken care of themselves and have been supported by others, it increases the chances that the baby will be born with an expectation of, "I am wanted."

Parent Tips for Healthy Pregnancy

- *A healthy pregnancy is the best start for a healthy baby.*

- *A complete avoidance of alcohol, illicit drugs and smoking is recommended.*

- *Supplementation of folic acid can reduce the chance of spina bifida in the baby.*

- *Babies can be born with emotional memory.*

- *Everyone needs to support pregnant women regardless of age, culture or social status.*

Providing for the nutritional requirements of the tribe
required the whole tribe. men often hunted the large prey
and then shared the meat with everyone else. Women and
children shared gathering seeds, nuts, fruits and smaller
protein foods like fish, lizards and small marsupials and
mammals. Food gathered was unprocessed, and largely fresh as
there was no way of preserving it as we know today. Food was
also a key element in tribal social gatherings, celebrations,
rituals and rites of passage.

Building Block 2
Good nutrition

It is essential that babies, toddlers and children have their nutritional and safety needs met. Primary carers need to make this a priority because babies and toddlers are completely dependent on them for food and drink.

> "Most of the chronic illnesses of today were either rare or unheard of just 100 years ago and still don't exist in many countries where people live on traditional diets. Unless we change now, the current generation of children will be the first to die at an earlier age than their parents."
>
> My Dog Eats Better than Your Kids, Dr Peter Dingle, 2008.

During pregnancy and the first two years of a child's life, adequate and healthy nutrition is critical. Recent studies in brain research show that good nutrition supports neuron development and improves mood and behaviour. The brain almost doubles in size in the first two years of life, so it is important to provide your baby with good nutrition.

> Learning restraint around the treats of life helps build a less self indulgent attitude to foods that should be eaten only in moderation. Young children are often unable themselves to make good health decisions, and early indulgence in the wrong foods can lead to obesity and poor health for life.

Top nutrition tips for babies, toddlers and children

- *Begin with mother's milk, if possible.*

- *Water is the best fluid for babies and toddlers, in addition to their breast milk or formula.*

- *Ensure sufficient protein for growing babies and toddlers.*

- *Avoid soft drinks until at least five years of age, and only then in limited amounts.*

- *Avoid cordials and fruit juice drinks that are high in sugar. Choose only pure fruit juice.*

- ***Never put sweet drinks, including sweet milk drinks and juice, into your baby's bottle.***

- *No deep-fried foods or fast foods like hamburgers, hot dogs and chips.*

- *Avoid potato chips, crisps and similar snacks.*

- *Avoid pre-packaged doughnuts, cakes, biscuits and pasties.*

- *Avoid unhealthy cereals that are low in fibre, high in sugar and salt.*

- *Avoid any foods with MSG (monosodium glutamate).*

- *Choose whole fruits.*

- *Choose wholegrain breads, fresh salads, lean meat, chicken or cheese.*

- *Choose preservative-free bread.*

- *Allow young children to graze on healthy foods, rather than eat according to adult meal times.*

- *Ensure children eat foods that provide essential fatty acids such as Omega 3 in oily fish, linseed, sunflower seeds and walnuts.*

- *Vitamin and mineral supplements (known as*

micronutrients) can be beneficial while children are growing—especially iodine, iron, zinc and vitamin B12.

- *Ensure children eat a breakfast that contains protein—the brain needs protein to function properly.*

- *Avoid sugary products, drinks and sweets in packed lunches.*

- *Keep lollies, chocolates and sweets to a minimum.*

- *Keep portions to a moderate size, regardless of age.*

- *Avoid negative environmental factors such as cigarette smoke, polluted air, mites, moulds and allergens, poisonous minerals like lead and mercury (found in some seafood including fish and mussels, dental amalgam, some medications, and pesticides and fungicides), and excessive electro-radiation (microwave ovens, mobile phones and overhead heavy-duty power lines).*

Studies on obesity show that being overweight is more the result of poor quality, nutritionally depleted foods eaten in large quantities than a lack of exercise. This is something that can be easily changed.

In my work as a therapist, I have found that children and teenagers who are struggling with obesity have a deep emotional wound hiding underneath. This is a problem that is seldom identified. The wound is comforted by eating, however it will keep on needing to be comforted until the problem is healed. Another layer of damage that has to be acknowledged is the shame that follows from being teased and abused for being fat.

Recent research shows that homes that have pets and a more relaxed approach to cleanliness have children with stronger immune systems, fewer allergies and less asthma. The consumerist world plays hard on products that are antibacterial and sweet smelling. Yet scientists can tell you that these products contain many harmful chemicals. Be careful not to be sucked in, there are cheaper and healthier alternatives for all forms of cleaning. I am a huge fan of the 'Queen of Clean', Shannon Lush. I value the return to many of my grandmother's tips for cleaning. Check out Lush's first book, *Spotless* and embrace her holistic cleaning when it is needed.

Additives and colourings are of great concern in how they may affect our children's lives. Many additives cause adverse reactions such as allergies, asthma, hyperactivity and rashes.

> Some of the dangerous designated numbers to avoid in foods are: 102, 4R, 124, 110, 122, 104, 129 and 211.

In a recent experiment carried out at the Nana Glen Public School on the north coast of New South Wales, students' diets were transformed—over 50 preservatives were removed from canteen and home lunches - for two weeks. The teachers were stunned with the changes in their students' behaviour:

"We noticed a huge change. The kids were more on task and the work they were producing was a lot better."

Good nutrition supports neuron development, increases brain integration, and improves mood and behaviour. It is essential to give our children the best chance to navigate our world by ensuring they eat foods that are good for them. This is one of the first building blocks that I explore when a troubled child with aggressive tendencies is referred to me. The second building block that I explore is building meaningful connections and the third is boundaries around sleep. Changing these three essentials can make a huge difference in a child's world. Their behaviour can change quickly and noticeably.

Remember that there is no place for large bottles of soft drink in a family's fridge with easy access by children and teenagers. Providing ready access to soft drinks is a form of child abuse because it sets them up for a life of needing this consumer driven, useless and damaging liquid for the rest of their lives. The same goes for junk food like crisps, chips and other packaged processed snack foods. If they are not available then your children and teenagers will have to eat something healthier—provided it is easily accessible!

Children have moments of exquisite joy and delight in a healthy childhood. These moments help the brain to develop an expectation that life can be fun. The experiences can also stimulate the pleasure seeking part of the brain. The pain seeking part of the brain develops without any help from a child's family—life itself can be challenging enough. Memories that are built around pleasurable moments in life—especially ones that are repeated, like bush barbecues, Christmas celebrations and birthday parties—are linked via our smell, visual and gustatory memories. The smell of a roast dinner, curry cooking, biscuits, or fresh bread being baked evoke instant feel-good endorphins for the rest of your life if you were happily exposed to them when you were a child. These can be positive ways to build a strong sense of caring connectedness in families, and they will help shift negative moods later in life. When food memories are linked to healthy food they will always create a positive mood or mind set and be good for you.

There are some scary 'food Nazis' in our world today who attack any food that is not organic, living and fresh. They attack any treat foods like cup cakes and biscuits because they contain sugar and fat. I am a huge believer in moderation and that children can learn which foods attract an 'occasional' label. This vital education ensures that parents can create special moments in their homes to celebrate important events. Treat foods are also better if they are prepared and baked at home using fresh eggs, wholemeal flour and less sugar than is found in items purchased from stores. Do you know what powdered eggs or milk solids look like? If its not real, it can't be good for you. Nothing is more fun than to have children help you make home-made biscuits for Nanna's birthday. There is so much other invisible emotional and social learning taking place during this hands on, meaningful experience.

Lack of sleep can be linked to poor mood control and

inappropriate behaviour. Sleep researchers have found that lack of sleep increases the body's yearning for junk food with its high levels of fat, salt and sugar. These help to soothe the pain-seeking mood that occurs without sufficient sleep. Researchers have also found that lack of sleep can increase the chances of gaining weight. When triggered often, the stress hormone cortisol actually stimulates the creation of fat cells to help create a sense of comfort.

Our fast-paced world has created marketing practices that disempower busy parents from providing nutritious food that nurtures the mind, body, heart and soul. Pre-packaged foods and instant meals are made in an economically viable way, which means using powdered eggs, excess salt, trans fatty acids and other shortcuts. These foods may be quick but are they worth it in the long term? Your children learn about the importance of 'quick' meals. That is very sad and nutritionally very bad news for their growing bodies. Food that is grown in alignment with the seasons is the very best food for you. It is created with the highest vibration energetically and is meant to be eaten fresh, not 12 months later when it comes out of storage. Organic food is obviously better for a family than commercially grown fruit and vegetables, however its cost is prohibitive for many families.

There has been a wonderful return to home vegetable patches. These not only provide seasonal vegetables, they also teach children a consciousness about nurturing oneself and others. I celebrate the Victorian kitchen garden project that Stephanie Alexander promotes. The schools building these gardens have created more than a change in eating patterns, they have built a community project that creates meaningful connections between staff, parents and students. Together they  learn to cook with fresh ingredients, and they have learned how to be both responsible and economically sustainable—something we are definitely going to need in the future.

The size of servings is something that has changed over the last

10-20 years. It is also encouraged to 'up-size' in many take away food outlets and this is something that shows how seductive advertising can be. Small portions were healthy and sustaining— and still can be. Restraint around how much our children are given to eat especially when it is food that should be occasional is the responsibility of parents. Be strong because there is no one sadder than a child in an obese body who gets teased mercilessly at school.

There is one last point about cooking healthy, tasty food at home with the whole family involved. There is one ingredient that goes into mum or dad's meal that cannot be purchased from the supermarket, and that's good old fashioned love! Children feel loved and valued when they eat food that has been prepared by a caring parent. Nothing will ever replace that essential part of good home nutrition.

> When children are given good quality food, and are given opportunities to learn about growing vegetables and fruit, they develop a consciousness about sustainability rather than a consumer mentality. Food that is prepared with love and then shared allows a child to learn another important reality that says, "I am cared for," and, "I am nurtured."

Parent tips around good nutrition

- *Patterns around food are created early in life.*

- *Good nutrition supports neuron development, increases brain integration, and improves mood and behaviour.*

- *Moderation is helpful around children.*

- *Food is linked to memory pathways and can influence us in adulthood.*

- *Eating together helps build connectedness.*

- *Learning restraint around the treats of life helps build a less self indulgent attitude to foods that should be eaten only in moderation.*

- *Involving children in the growing and preparation of food is helpful to develop healthy nutritional habits for life.*

- *Occasional treats can build positive human celebrations.*

Within traditional tribal communities babies seldom leave their mothers' sides. A mother sleeps beside her baby and often carries the baby while she works. She has a close, extended family that also supports her growing baby through infanthood. Children play freely in the vicinity of the women of the tribe and help with simple tasks like gathering fruit and seeds and carrying water. The circle of family can include non-biological members and it is seen as the whole tribe's responsibility to take care of growing children until puberty, when boys and girls are then prepared for adulthood.

Building Block 3
Safe, nurturing care within the family circle

> We can love in peace or torment. Loving in peace means that you associate love with deep states of well being. Loving in torment means peaks of excitement marred with jealousy, destructive rage and fears of both dependency and abandonment. Whether your child will love in peace or love in torment will be profoundly, influenced by the way you love your child now, and the brain chemistries and systems activated as a result.
>
> Margot Sunderland, The Science of Parenting,2006

Babies and toddlers have a strong, instinctive drive for safety, closeness and forming relationships with people. These close connections are essential for building resilience, and early relationships are most beneficial when they are in the presence of genuine, loving care. Both fathers and mothers are important. If this is not possible, deep connections to significant carers will bring the same benefits. It is the loving care of young babies and toddlers that shapes the developing neural pathways, rather than the biological linkage.

Extreme neglect or deprivation in the first year of life, where a baby is rarely touched, soothed or talked to, impacts on the baby's emotional and mental strength. These babies have difficulty in coping later in life. Mothering skills can be learned and every community needs to be as supportive as possible to both new mums, and mums of new babies. Social isolation and lack of support may create serious challenges for mothers of babies and young children.

> Adequate nurturing and the absence of intense early stress permit our brains to develop in a manner that is less aggressive and more emotionally stable, social and empathetic.
>
> *The Neurobiology of Child Abuse,* Martin Teicher, *Scientific American* (March 2002).

Being able to provide a close, nurturing environment for babies builds the parents' capacity to better understand the needs of their growing baby. Babies and toddlers like to feel safe and to form relationships with people. It is the babies who have a healthy sense of attachment to their primary carers who are most curious and explore more freely. Through their experiences, babies and children are continuously interpreting others and the world around them. Caring adults provide babies with a secure base from which they can explore and interpret life experiences, without smothering or over controlling them. I have been impressed with the wonderful work of Jenny Roberts called *Kidscode*. In this process Jenny teaches parents how to give themselves calmness and space to allow children to be children and to give them the capacity to use what they were born with—creativity and curiosity. Her work with families with children who are on the autistic spectrum has shown that even these children

can learn for themselves, rather than always needing to be taught. She is currently conducting a research project to show this.

Researchers in the field of early childhood development have recently explored 'the secure base'. They followed the pattern of behaviour of infants and babies and noticed that secure babies with a healthy sense of attachment to their mothers were able to explore freely and focus on their environment, while keeping an eye on their mother. When mothers left their babies for a short time and then returned, the researchers found different patterns of responses by the different babies. Some sought their mothers out immediately and then returned to playing; these would seem to be the secure babies. Other babies expressed great distress and anger and could not be comforted, or they pulled away and were indifferent to their mother's return; these were the less secure babies.

Constant rejection can create a deep sense of emotional insecurity and distrust of others. The rejection impacts on a child's ability to make deep, lasting friendships later in life—an important protective element and one of the building blocks for developing resilience. Nothing can replace this crucial need to develop a positive attachment to a primary carer, a person who genuinely cares about the child.

> Our effectiveness as parents will be in direct proportion to the strength of the connection we have with our child.
>
> *Connection Parenting,* Pam Leo, *Kindred Magazine* (June-August 2008).

Margot Sunderland in her book, *The Science of Parenting* expresses her concern about the impact of separation anxiety in babies and infants, and the long term effects this can have. Separation hurts young children in much the same way as physical pain, and can still be influencing children who are as old as 10 years of age. The brain's GABA (gamma-aminobutyric acid) system is very sensitive to environmental changes. These changes include both separation from a parent and social dislocation, such as a change of home, school or primary carer. To soothe a baby or infant who is distressed Sunderland recommends these three key comforts:

1. Touch and massage, to activate oxytocins release.
2. Sucking, preferably a fist or a thumb.
3. Warmth, as this releases oxytocin as well.

> With emotionally responsive parenting vital connections will form in the baby's brain enabling him to cope with stress in later life; form fulfilling relationships; manage anger well; be kind and compassionate; have the will and the motivation to follow his ambitions and his dreams; experience the deepest calm; love intimately and in peace.
>
> *The Science of Parenting*, Margot Sunderland (2006).

Family, friends, regular outings and community support networks, like playgroups and walking groups, are very beneficial in the first two years of a baby's life. They offer additional interactions for the baby and respite for the primary carer. Parents will not always be able to provide every social need for their growing baby, and exhausted parents are less likely to have energy to play games or interact with a toddler. Games and activities build pathways to a child's ability to learn basic literacy skills later on when he or she is at school. Respite is recognised as being essential in raising young children. An exhausted parent usually needs about one to two hours of respite to completely refill their heart with love for their child—provided someone they trust cares for their child during that time. Parenting can be a very tiring, frustrating and repetitive journey when travelled without support.

Consciously creating a circle of support for young children ensures that they are exposed to holistic experiences that build healthy children. Some things that help them are:

- *modelling unconditional love and care*
- *allowing children the space 'to be'*
- *being truthful and honest*
- *creating a safe place for them to share their emotions*
- *being a positive dreamer and goal setter yourself*
- *being real, not perfect or a know-it-all*
- *being joyful and laughing often*
- *having clear, firm boundaries*
- *modelling personal health and well-being*
- *being connected to your own spirit*
- *having relationships that you value and nurture.*

> Allow them to feel connected and valued in their families, friendships, schools, communities and in our natural wide world. An article in *The West Australian* newspaper (October 22nd 2005, p62) showed that kids are likely to rate a hug from mum as of higher importance than the latest X-Box game. Special education and behaviour management lecturer Jonathon Sargeant from New England University found in his PhD study 'cuddles, affection and happy parents' were high on the list of what pleased children the most.
>
> *Nurturing Kids Hearts and Souls*, Maggie Dent (2005).

The safe circle provides opportunities to support the healthy development of babies and toddlers. The things that worked in the past, before our modern technological world, still allow healthy development. This includes child-centred learning experiences rather than adult-driven ones. Babies do not need massive, expensive machine-made toys or DVDs to be stimulated. The natural world is fascinating for growing babies and toddlers, especially with things like baskets of clothes pegs (or pins), coloured paper, the plastics cupboard, cuddly comfort teddies and stuffed animals.

Babies need repeated experiences in which they can self-direct and build the neural connections in the brain that create memory. When children are bored they are wired to move on to something else, to continue to engage their inquisitive brains. Learning how to manage boredom is a vital stage of development that over-stimulated babies and children need to master. When adults over-direct an infant's learning, with noisy toys, screens and even educational DVDs, they run a serious risk of invalidating the baby's natural curiosity and also causing the baby hidden stress. Early over-stimulation causes the baby's brain to flood with stress hormones, which can cause them to be distressed and it can hard wire them to be overly sensitive to stress for the rest of their lives. Dr Bruce Perry has studied the chronic damage that happens to a child's neurological system from abuse and neglect.

> "While each child has unique genetic potentials, both human and animal studies point to important needs that every child has, and severe long-term consequences for brain function if those needs are not met. The effects of the childhood environment, favourable or unfavourable, interact with all the processes of neurodevelopment."
>
> Childhood Experience and the Expression of Genetic Potential,
> Dr Bruce D Perry

This safe circle is a vital building block in all children's lives. It is preferable if it is the biological family, however as "safe, nurturing" is what the developing baby's brain must experience to develop the neural pathways that ensure emotional and psychological well being as an adult, this is more important than having a common gene pool.

This circle has the enormous responsibility of providing a healthy, interesting environment for the baby and toddler to experience. Children who sit and watch many hours of TV have two main challenges. The first is that the visual over-stimulation increases their stress levels. There are over 400 research studies showing that children who watch programs that contain aggression will themselves become more aggressive. These same studies show that over-exposure to TV increases the chances of children developing attention-deficit hyperactivity disorder (ADHD) and other hyperactivity disorders. The second concern is that watching TV is a passive activity and inhibits natural inquisitiveness and seeking that a growing brain needs. Children's little brains become numb and lazy; this is at a time when babies and toddlers have the potential to learn massively, quickly and efficiently.

Another serious issue with the over-use of TV is exposure to commercials. The advertising world is keen to grab, as soon as possible, your baby or toddler's "I want" mentality. Once the commercial has built a passive belief that a product will make a child happy, it is with them for life. Avoid TV use for any child less than two years of age, and if necessary use non-commercial TV programs. Use the natural world and you will have a calmer and smarter toddler! After two years of age limited use of quality programs and DVDs, without commercials, will continue to help your toddler learn in an optimal way.

> There is no substitute for REAL experiences with real people, doing real things and exploring the real world.

The research studies that showed the potential danger of screens in young children' lives were conducted when TV screens were normal sized. Common sense suggests that very large plasma screens and home theatres would have to be amplifying the over-stimulation. Is it any wonder that Ritalin prescriptions have risen from 11,500 in 1994 to over 210,000 in 2006 in Australia? We have a culture in the Western world where:

> Keeping the natural world out of the reach of children seems to be our national passion. In fact greater numbers of children are brought up in the artificial world of cement, asphalt, plastics and the virtual reality of television while fewer each year experience a world of nature and the unfolding of organic life.
>
> The Biology of Transcendence: A Blueprint of the Human Spirit, Joseph Chilton Pearce, 2004.

I totally salute this view and urge parents, grandparents and carers to allow children to explore the natural world with the vim and vigour that is encoded in their genes. Allow them to experience the exquisite moments of joy when jumping in puddles, diving into piles of Autumn leaves, feeding (with appropriate wild feed) ducks in a local lake, catching tadpoles and making mud pies as only children can. These are the experiences that children are meant to have so that they can better cope with the adult world of responsibility and stress when it does arrive. I was writing this chapter when I received an email from a mother who recently attended my seminar on building resilience in children. In the email she shared a loving detour from her busy life that she had taken with her three children:

"I took your advice and after I collected the children from school today we went to the beach and walked and explored and played. We came home calmer, happier and the night flowed smoothly—so simple and natural. Thank you."

As adults our responsibility is to create safe, interesting environments and then to let the kids do the rest. Mildly enriching their environments does not mean buying expensive educational toys, it means adding a wooden spoon to their sand play or a whisk while they explore the plastics cupboard. In education it is sometimes called 'scaffolding'. Early years specialist Magda Gerber described this technique to mean that a caregiver keeps an eye out for a situation that has the potential for learning. The adult then takes the opportunity to sensitively and respectfully structure the situation so that a new conversation or problem solving opportunity is encouraged and supported. For example, if a child spilled their juice the carer helps the child explore what had happened. Was it too full? Would a lid on the cup have helped prevent the spill? Were they walking too fast? This enabled the child to see solutions rather than problems in life's everyday experiences.

> Children are not problems to be solved.
> Children are solutions waiting to be found.

Associate Professor Margaret Sims from Edith Cowan University explained that the idea of play was for children to explore and experiment with their surroundings so they could see how things worked and to observe cause and affect relationships in the world (*The West Australian,* 22 October 2005, p62).

A safe circle of support and care provides simple connections between a carer and their baby, toddler or child. Fathers are vitally important in this circle and may need to be encouraged when they are first time fathers. Simple activities like reading favourite picture books, reciting nursery rhymes, and playing hand and clapping

games all build fun and smart brains. Real experiences are trips to the beach or the park, helping in the garden with grandad, helping nanna bake biscuits, and feeding the chooks. The child learns how to be useful. Given the chance to explore their mildly stimulating world within the protective safety of people who care about them, children develop emotional, social and spiritual competence. These competencies stay with them for life.

Some vital things happen when children are read to yet these may go unnoticed by adults. Reading books to your young children every day can help them:

- *develop a love of books and reading*
- *develop imagination, creativity and exploration skills*
- *strengthen brain pathways and memory, enhance brain development and recall of language*
- *develop an understanding of text and the meaning and mechanics of language*
- *develop vocabulary and comprehension*
- *enhance their curiosity*
- *stimulate themselves in multi-sensory ways*
- *form a bond with a caring adult*
- *enjoy a calming activity that is largely still*
- *build a strong foundation so that they can become successful readers for life.*

An excellent Australian book that parents can use at home to enhance their children's pre-literacy skills is, *Up Down: A Fun and Practical Way to Introduce Reading and Writing to Children aged 2–5* by Michelle Neumann. This is not to be used in the form of accelerated learning, rather Michelle explores many of the early pathways to literacy. I enjoy her air-drawing letters activity, it brought back memories of drawing letters and numbers on my sons' backs. They loved the tickle as well as the game aspect.

Another excellent book is, *Infants, Toddlers and Caregiver* by Janet Gonzalez-Mena and Dianne Widmeyer Eyer. The very simple recommendation for parents and carers is to involve infants and toddlers in things that concern them. The understanding is that when a child participates in the experience with her caregiver rather than being the recipient, her learning will be of value. This book explores the work of the Hungarian paediatrician Emmi Pikler who was a strong advocate for respectful interaction with children. I find the information refreshing and very organic, much like the way that traditional communities approached the role of raising children. Dr Pikler and her key advocates, especially Magda Gerber, believe that the following principles apply to raising and caring for infants and toddlers.

10 principles based on a philosophy of respect

1. *Involve infants and toddlers in things that concern them.*

2. *Invest in quality time, when you are totally available to individual infants and toddlers.*

3. *Learn each child's unique ways of communicating and also teach yours—don't underestimate children's ability to communicate even though their verbal language skills may be nonexistent or minimal.*

4. *Invest time and energy to build a total person— concentrate on the whole child.*

5. *Respect infants and toddlers as worthy people. Don't treat them as objects or cute little empty headed people to be manipulated.*

6. *Be honest with your feelings.*

7. *Model the behaviour you want to teach.*

8. *Recognise problems as learning opportunities and let infants and toddlers try to solve their own problems. Don't rescue them, constantly make life easy for them or protect them from all problems.*

9. *Build security by building trust. Don't teach distrust by being undependable or frequently inconsistent.*

10. *Be concerned about the quality of development in each stage. Don't rush infants and toddlers to reach developmental milestones.*

The key points are:

Respectful–Responsive–Reciprocal–Interaction

This approach encompasses the whole child rather than a sum of a number of parts. It also acknowledges that all children are unique—some children develop faster in certain areas, while in other areas they may be delayed. This is not seen as a problem, merely a reflection on the unique journey of a toddler or child. The authors of the principles have a clear expectation that with quality care, which is responsive and respectful of each individual child, they will grow on all levels. This approach does not have a prescribed list of targets that children should meet at certain ages; it simply honours children to grow and develop in alignment with their innate pathways while being surrounded by caring, aware adults.

Unfortunately, some education systems test children when they are as young as four years of age. This is of enormous concern on many levels. Early labels like 'poor listening skills' or 'low attention ability' or 'hyperactivity' can stay with children for life. Early testing runs against the recommendations of mainstream early years educators who have been involved in education of young children for many years. Good early years care can create environments in which children are given learning opportunities where they develop quality, respectful caring relationships with adults—those who are comfortable with a holistic, grounded approach to education.

> Be careful about falling into the trap of thinking that you can stimulate cognitive development without working on physical, social and emotional development at the same time. It isn't the clever little toys that you provide or the activities that you do with children that make a difference. It's the day to day living, the relationships, the experiences, the daiperings, the feedings, the toilet training, and the playing that contribute to intellectual development. And those same experiences help the child grow physically, socially and emotionally as well.
>
> *Infants, Toddlers and Caregivers: The Philosophy of Respect Based on the Work by Magda Gerber and the Hungarian Paediatrician Emmi Pikler,* Gonzalez-Mena, Janet and Widmeyer Eyer, Dianne (2006).

It is important that parents and carers of children resist the hurried world we now live in. Nature has provided the means to support babies to become healthy children for over five million years without needing to hurry them. Many modern parents appear to interpret this ancient art of parenting as a strange journey, as though it is a competition. There is a serious danger that 'kid-pushing' can be very detrimental to a child's growth, especially psychologically and if he or she develops a premature sense of failure of, "I am dumb".

> Children are pushed, pushed, pushed. When adults have this hurry up attitude babies are propped up before they can sit on their own, walked around by the hand before they can even stand by themselves, taught to ride a tricycle when they can barely walk.
>
> Gonzalez-Mena et al.

Another advocate for the unhurried approach to raising children is Australian education consultant Kathy Walker. She argues that there is now less time for children to play. This follows an explosion of extra-curricular activities, organised sports, athletic programs and dance and movement classes. Many childcare workers express concerns that they find more and more children who are too tired to play or who wait to be organised into prescribed activities. Some over-zealous parents want a young child's pasting creation to look like something recognisable, rather than seeing the creation as a vital stage of development where the child has learned to master scissors, the glue pot, concepts of shape and size and how to stay focused on a task. These hidden purposes are enormous in the child's world and often not appreciated by well-meaning parents.

> Children who are over scheduled into weekly activities may inadvertently be learning that life is about having every moment of their lives filled with entertainment and prescribed activities. Consequently, opportunities to show initiative, play alone and/or create experiences for themselves appear to have become lost.
>
> *What's The Hurry: Reclaiming Childhood in an Overscheduled World*, Kathy Walker, (2005).

We must never forget that child development cannot be hurried, no matter how inconvenient that may be for the adults of our 'hurry up' world. Each child has a built-in timetable that dictates just when he or she will crawl, sit up and start to walk; and given a safe environment, their development flows naturally. A key aspect to remember is that a child's important learning milestones and developmental growth come **when the baby is ready, not when the adult decides it is time.**

Please pause for a moment to read the last sentence again; and then reflect. I firmly believe that much of the stress and anxiety present in children's lives comes from hidden pressures and overzealous expectations of well-meaning parents, and sometimes teachers. Adults want to hurry up the innate and

unique development of children in a busy, instant world. Albert Einstein was very delayed in his development and was mainly non-verbal as a young child. He later became one of the world's smartest and wisest scientists. I wonder what would have happened if he had been born in today's hurried world?

Creating and maintaining a safe environment is crucial in raising happy and healthy children. It is important that everyone in the community is committed to protecting and nurturing our children. Be brave if your extended family lives a long way from your young family, find some good people nearby and invite them to support you. Everyone can win in that situation because there are many older people who have a lot of time on their hands. Some live lonely lives and they may love to share the journey of your young family. The more support parents of young children can get the more they will enjoy this sometimes challenging journey in our busy, chaotic world.

Recommendations for yourself and the care of very young children

- Become informed about babyhood and early childhood before becoming pregnant.

- Take care of your physical and emotional needs during pregnancy.

- Create as much time as possible to mothering and caring for your newborn.

- Create a supportive network before your baby arrives.

- Become securely attuned to your baby's needs.

- Avoid child care outside the home for as long as possible— the less time infants spent in day care the better.

- Be aware that toddlers under two years of age may not be able to socialise easily.

- Avoid using the TV as a babysitter.

- Avoid too many toys.

- Avoid too much talking and coaching.

- Long term effects of extensive child care—more than 30 hours per week—can cause problem behaviours, especially those associated with anxiety, aggression and oppositional behaviour.

- Committed parents sharing child care of young children in their own home is preferable to outside child care of babies and toddlers under two years of age.

- Carers of children need to be chosen on the grounds of their capacity to provide loving care—safe, gentle touch, soothing words, capacity to reassure and time to do so.

- Become informed about the key issues in outside child care. Enquire about ratios of staff to children, how staff manage challenging behaviours, fussy eaters and anxious children. Check on the staff turnover.

- Family-based child care is better than having the children together en masse if the above concerns are explored. A familiar place with a consistent carer builds security for toddlers.

- Trained nannies in the home who meet the above concerns, and who become a part of the family network, offer a positive alternative to outside child care.

The importance of strong communities

Caring neighbourhoods and communities build a strong sense in a child of their being noticed, accepted and valued by others. The spirit of relationships that strengthen a community are created through the four 'Cs' of:
- Community
- Connection
- Compassion
- Communion.

Communities that practise these four qualities build healthy adults. They see raising children as a privilege and take pride in helping the children grow up to become healthy adults. Connectedness occurs when people feel they belong, are accepted unconditionally and know that their community watches over them regardless of their age, state of health and vulnerabilities.

Community fetes and festival days are ideal opportunities to build spirit and to celebrate together, both as a family and a community. In rural Australia there are a great variety of events throughout the year. These include jazz festivals, flower festivals, agricultural shows or expositions, wine and food shows, craft shows, antique fairs, school reunions, country music events and even 'dog in a ute' gatherings. They are all opportunities for special interest groups to meet with visitors coming to their communities to find fellowship and fun. The events are successful financially, socially and spiritually. Strong, positive-thinking communities come together for celebration and also in times of need and tragedy. Sometimes it takes a crisis to re-awaken a community to the importance of being connected. The stronger the community is then the more powerful is the response to any crisis or adversity. Remember that strong communities raise healthy, resilient children, just as traditional tribal villages did. Crime is reduced when people value and respect the environment in which they live. People are valued and in turn they value others and their property. Here are some suggestions and recommendations that can help to strengthen communities.

Since the beginning of mankind people have been involved in birthing, raising children and dying. People have not always had university trained professionals, counsellors, medical equipment and drugs, cars, washing machines, mobile phones and computers available to them. They have not always had consumerism, technology and globalisation. In times gone by, the main purpose in life was to continue the species and survive. To achieve this people worked beside each other, for each other, and for the future of their children. They accepted responsibility for the type of adult a child became and they placed the holistic growth of their children as their number one priority.

Children need a safe circle of support within a community that values them to be given the best opportunity to grow up healthy, happy and resilient. Life is seldom smooth and conflict free. The more tools we develop over the years to help us bounce back then the better quality of life we can have. Resilience is often more evident in people who have been able to overcome tough experiences. They have shown they have the capacity to get up, get back into life and let the past stay where it is—in the past. Resilience is something we can help our children to learn and develop. Over-protecting children from pain and disappointment does not help them in developing effective protective mechanisms, or the mental and physical toughness for living life. This is why it takes a whole village to raise a child. It is why the return to a family and a community model of raising our children is important.

Parent Tips to build safe circle of family

- *Babies brains are shaped by the early experiences of loving care or deprivation and abuse*

- *Safe circles of support for families with young children are very important*

- *Avoid hurrying childhood – it takes time, love and lots of energy*

- *Avoid the technological world*

- *Avoid overstimulating young babies and children*

- *Play in the natural world builds healthy bodies and minds*

- *Avoid over protecting children from making mistakes*

- *Make decisions about child care very carefully*

- *Young children get distressed easily with change or lack of contact with key care givers*

- *Strong community involvement helps families raise healthy children.*

- *Don't rush infants and toddlers to reach developmental milestones*

In traditional communities, infants and children played freely, mainly in the vicinity of the women. They played in the company of children of varying ages, and the older children learned to interact, take care of and be responsible for the smaller children.

Free play, which we call unstructured play, involved dirt, trees, puddles and lots of mud and sand. It was a vital aspect of childhood. Adults were too busy providing food, shelter and safety to be directing or organising their children's play activities. During their playtime adventures children were sometimes injured or hurt, and this was seen as a normal part of childhood. Real experience was how children learnt about themselves, others and the world they lived in.

Traditional tribes avoided 'shouldering' their children they believed that a child would only ever pick up a hot coal once. In other words, real experience is often the best teacher! Children-at-play was a valued part of a community and children were encouraged to be independent and non-directed in their play.

Building Block 4
Plenty of play

> We have failed a generation of
> children and continue to do so.
>
> Dr George Halasz, Melbourne, Australia.

Australia's *Herald Sun* reported that a survey by *The Advertiser* of more than 50 public (state) primary schools in south Australia revealed playtime has been reduced to as low as 15 minutes in some schools to combat poor behaviour and in some cases, violence. Instead of 40 minutes of playtime, many students are now given a 10 minute sit-down lunch and only 30 minutes of play (July 7, 2008). The revelations follow concerns from Deakin University researcher, Dr Gwenda Davey who warns Australians could follow the lead of the USA and abolish playtime completely because of fears of violence, injury and litigation. This news is deeply concerning.

When I spent time with Jenny Mosley of Circle time fame in the United Kingdom she showed that if children do not have enough time to initiate games, there can be problems. Also as today's children lose the knowledge of how to play games, especially simple, traditional games that do not require a screen, they will struggle to connect and play more. Schools need to recognise the value of games and play in the healthy development of children—no matter how curriculum driven the pressures have become. Frustrated children will cause problems, while children who have fun with play won't.

Early years educators and child care specialists know the importance of plenty of play for early child development. Play stimulates physical development, social and emotional growth. Play is also a fun way to build early brain integration, which is needed for literacy and life-long learning. With the increase in psychological, emotional and social problems and disorders in Western Australian children in the last 10 years (*Health Commission of Western Australia Report 2003-2004*) the role of play has been re-examined. Its importance is reaffirmed as being essential for well-being and resilience.

Children are biologically wired to play. Play is very serious business for them. Opportunities for play are essential because they help a child learn many of the emotional and social competencies. These cannot be developed through direct verbal interaction with adults. Solo play, parallel play and interactive play are all healthy forms of play for children to experience in childhood.

It is alarming that there is actually a condition called 'tactile defensiveness' that is coming into our modern world, where children appear in preschool without the social and emotional skills to interact with other children. Some schools in the UK have nurture groups created to overcome such circumstances. This is sad, but true.

There appears to be a serious gap occurring in children's early years which is delaying emotional and social development. This has a lot to do with the changing nature of modern childhoods. The excess consumer-driven pressures on parents to buy toys and 'stuff' to make their children smart has, in part, invalidated the magic that is wired into children that leads them to find their own fun. Just because a product has "educational " written on it's packaging, does not mean that it has any more educational value than a basket of clothes pegs or a set of car keys to a young toddler! The real world is full of stimulation for babies and toddlers and that includes dirty marks in the carpet and even dried kangaroo poo, as one of my sons discovered!

Children learn a lot from exploring their world without bells, whistles and batteries. To toddlers there is enormous learning to be found in a simple things that occur in almost all homes - pegs, cellophane paper and the plastics cupboard. Learning requires repeated and sequential experiences to create the neuronal connections for learning and development. It looks as boring as the proverbial bat poo to an adult, however to the toddler these activities are both stimulating and interesting. Almost everything young children do is some form of play.

Vital brain growth is occurring without the child experiencing stress from being over-stimulated or overly adult-directed. It is helpful to remember that the human brain is wired to learn, explore the hidden patterns of the world and to learn how to be a social being. Early autonomy that children find in play is very helpful in children's lives; this allows them to make some decisions for themselves and begin the journey towards personal responsibility and the art of making choices.

Children need real people to learn from about how to be social beings, not virtual beings. A study was done where a Sesame Street program was shown to a group of four year olds. The audio was replaced with the soundtrack from a different program. The little children sat passively for 40 minutes, even though the program was nonsense. They were numbed by the screen. It would seem that watching the TV screen can starve their imagination and stop them thinking and interacting with other people. This may be a contributing factor to the tactile defensiveness turning up in school children.

Physically passive pastimes, such as those involving audiovisual technology of TV, computer games and DVDs, can over-stimulate growing minds and cause stress levels to rise. Reliance on screen-based technology as babysitters has seen children develop a sense of immediacy and an in an instant mindset. Many children can drive a remote control better than ride bikes or build sand castles!

> In homes where there is heavy TV use children are less likely
> to read every day; and when they do read they tend to read
> for much shorter times. These children are the most likely
> group to not read at all.
>
> *Zero to Six: Electronic Media in the lives of Infants and Toddlers and
> Preschoolers*, A Kaiser Foundation Report, V. Rideout and E. Vandewater
> (2003).

Increasing levels of hyperactivity in children and the problems
caused by poor attention are often linked with excessive
exposure to television, especially in children aged 0–5 years
(DA. Christakis, FJ. Zimmerman, DL. Digiuesppe and CA.
McCarty (2004), *Early Television Exposure and Subsequent
Attentional Problems in Children*).

It is easy for children to access fictionalised negative portrayals
of life, with scenes and programs that involve violence, distress,
bad language, disrespect, fear and poor role models. These
shape a young child's emerging brain and challenge their
chances of developing a positive attitude to, and an optimistic
anticipation for, life. The TV news also provides children with the
global reality of terrorist attacks, wars and natural disasters. This
can create heightened fear about a child's own personal safety.
Children under 10 years of age benefit from being protected from
these media images. The most common sense answer to these
concerns is – be vigilant about TV usage and monitor it.
Remember your baby or toddlers brain grows 90% in the first 5
years of it's life – why fill it with rubbish and distortions or fill it
with perceptions that increase their interpersonal patterns of
behaviour. The studies done on TV's that showed these
disturbing trends were done on normal sized TV's and not the
large plasma and HD screens available today. What are these
massive screens doing to today's babies and toddlers sensitive
brains?

Much of the play equipment that was in the playgrounds when
we grew up has now been removed because they are believed to
be unsafe. These include the tall monkey bars, wooden see-saws
and the metal may-poles—equipment that had to be treated with

deep respect because you could seriously hurt yourself. Did you ever get thumped in the chin when someone jumped on the other end of the see-saw? Has your bum-been thumped when someone suddenly jumped off the see-saw? Well it only needed to happen once or twice to you before you treated the equipment with the respect it deserved. It seems that today's largely safe playgrounds are the product of our risk-averse society, where things are built to prevent children getting hurt.

Tim Gill, in his book, *No Fear: Growing Up in a Risk Averse Society* explores the long lasting effects in the UK of removing risk from childhood.

> Activities and experiences that previous generations enjoyed without a second thought have been labelled as troubling or dangerous, while adults who still permit them are branded as irresponsible... society appears to have become unable to cope with any adverse outcomes whatsoever, no matter how trivial or improbable.
>
> *No Fear: Growing up in a Risk Averse Society*, Tim Gill (2007).

Hugh Cunningham is Emeritus Professor of Social History at the University of Kent. His book, *The Invention of Childhood* shows that he too shares Tim Gill's concerns. Cunningham believes that society in general has become so fixated on ensuring children are happy that we downplay their abilities and their resilience. Taking up the debate about our collective responsibility for shaping childhood, he is now an activist and lobbyist in the UK who works to ensure that children's opportunities to play and have free time without adult supervision are not forever lost.

Tim Gill says today's parents spend much more time than previous generations in looking after their children. Parents are also constantly in touch with their children with mobile phones. The long-term effects of such strong structuring, supervision and control of the children on capacity to develop resilience is a key element of Gill's book. Children learn by being able to manage their own worlds, including the risks they encounter, with large developmental benefits. Some children's experts claim that a child can build on his or her character and personality through facing up to adverse circumstances, where there is a known possibility of injury or loss. At the same time, the child learns about the qualities of being adventuresome and innovative. Overcoming challenging situations is a key aspect of resilience and there is only one way to learn about it, and that is through experience. One school banned the game of tag because of the risk of injury. A student wrote the following response:

To be honest, adults can be very stupid at times. They ban everything, for health and safety reasons. If they're going to ban very simple stuff like this, they might as well lock all kids in empty rooms to keep them safe. Kids should be allowed to experiment and try things. Otherwise they will grow up and they'll make stupid mistakes from not getting enough experience at childhood (BBC website, 2005).

A key driver for the over-concern of those who care for children is the threat of litigation. This is one of the unfortunate side effects of the modern world. The litigation threat has shaped so much of the harm minimisation that impacts on children's playgrounds and school activities. It seems that accidents no longer happen, where a child or indeed an adult injures him or herself because they were inattentive, careless or simply distracted. Instead, someone or something must be to blame. This may be the manufacturer, the gardener who wet the path or the slide that simply became too hot on a very sunny day. The need to blame external sources is surely delaying the development of emotional competence, of accepting responsibility for one's own actions, both of which could have serious repercussions later in life. As a former teacher I can still remember how refreshing it was to have a student own up to being a source of conflict or inappropriate behaviour. Ironically, I usually let them go to recess or lunch early to honour the importance of being honest and able to accept personal responsibility.

Gill writes of how children of times gone by learned to take care and manage risks, because they knew that playgrounds were potentially dangerous. Today, children believe that playgrounds are safe and so they take little care and do not learn healthy risk assessment or management. This is commonly known as 'risk compensation'.

An Australian health professional validated this perspective for me when he told me that the number of children who suffer broken wrists nowadays is more than the number who broke their arms on monkey bars. The monkey bars were an excellent way of strengthening children's wrists and forearms. This is a beautiful example of how children learned to manage the bumps and bruises of life, because they had opportunities to do so. They were not mollycoddled and wrapped in cotton wool. Accidents were seen as a part of a healthy childhood, and not a sign of poor

parenting. Resilience is built from experiences of managing the things that can hurt physically, emotionally and psychologically.

At a seminar, a teacher shared with me that the monkey bars also provided an excellent opportunity for children who struggled academically to experience competence. The king or queen of the monkey bars had something that he or she could do and feel capable about. This is a key aspect of self esteem and builds a healthy sense of self. Tim Gill also explored what happened in the UK when impact absorbing surfaces became mandatory. Firstly, the cost of the new, safer surfaces was prohibitive and many playgrounds closed or they had fewer play items. Then evidence emerged that these rubber-like surfaces may be causing *more* broken arms than other types of surfaces (David Yearley, Head of Play Ground Safety, Royal Society for the Prevention of Accidents, Somerset Forum Conference, November 2006).

In the German city of Freiburg an interesting phenomenon has been taking place. In the 1990s the city began installing public playgrounds that made extensive use of slopes, logs, boulders, plants, sand and other natural features. Tim Gill met with the Freiburg Director of Parks, Harald Rabhein in 2005. He asked

Rabhein about playground safety in these more naturalistic playgrounds.

> Clearly there are more hazards and they are more varied, in natural play spaces compared to traditional play areas. In general children learn to take more care and responsibility for their safety in the natural play spaces and as a result, accident rates have not increased.
>
> Tim Gill.

When I ask a parent group what play they experienced as a child, and what they had really loved, an interesting thing happens. These parents do not mention expensive toys or indoor games. The things they had loved as kids were building cubbies, riding bikes (often without helmets, gears or brakes), catching tadpoles, building billy carts, climbing trees, and hours of chasey, hide-and-seek and spot-light. One parent shared that they used to go camping with their children at a beach campsite where they could have up to 30 children playing spot-light at night. Mind you, some of those children were in their 40s! These play pursuits would occur often and with little direction from adults and *cost very little money.*

The fun aspects of play serve an important role in developing a child's psychology. The more pleasurable experiences that a child has, the more chance they have of developing a pleasure-seeking response to unknown experiences. The opposite can also occur, where the more painful experiences the child has, the more likely it is that they will seek pain rather than pleasure out of new experiences. This becomes an unconscious process that happens quite spontaneously. It is influenced by the core concepts that a child has come to believe (J. Joseph (2005), *Learning in the Emotional Rooms: How to create classrooms that are uplifting for the spirit*, Focus Education Australia, Pty Ltd).

Important brain development takes place as a child plays. Some of that development requires tumbling, spinning, balancing and rolling, because it stimulates the sensory system. These activities help develop the cerebellum. Studies have shown that children with dyslexia and ADHD often have under-developed cerebellums, leading to poor sensory processing, inattention and hyperactivity. A group of children playing in a natural environment naturally balance, roll, spin and tumble. There is very little opportunity for these essential activities to occur when a child sits on a couch.

From around two years of age toddlers are capable of learning social skills that strengthen their life coping skills. The toddlers, starting to develop their sense of 'self', have the opportunity to develop autonomy and personal independence. The stronger a person's sense of identity and independence, together with the life skills to support these attributes, the better their resilience.

The parts of the brain that regulate emotion and attitudes to human relations require human contact to develop. Only real interactions build emotional competencies. These cannot be learned by watching a screen. Socialising is an excellent way for toddlers to develop and, although rigidly organised activities with adult intervention may seem beneficial to cognitive development, self-initiated play is often better. I have fond memories of my four sons playing for hours in the sandpit. They would make many strange noises without exchanging any real words. They had a fun time and, with hindsight, were learning vital 'boy codes' of communication—never waste words when strange grunts can suffice!

Children have an enormous curiosity and thirst for life when exploring their world, especially when they are with other children. Curiosity and innovative, flexible thinking are strong attributes of resilient people. Margot Sunderland in her book, *The Science of Parenting* writes about the importance of developing the mammalian brain, especially the areas associated with caring and nurturing, social bonding, playfulness and the explorative urge. This last attribute, also called the seeking system, is like a muscle—the more you use it the more it develops. In humans this system can activate an appetite for life, an energy to explore the new and an eagerness to seek out the fruits of the world. It also stimulates our curiosity, absorbed interest and sustained motivation to achieve our goals. This is what free play and child-centred activity helps to nurture in a child's brain. Maybe the mind numbing influence of TV and play within adult centred worlds is crushing this vital brain development. This may make an individual susceptible to mental illnesses such as depression, and have a poor motivation for life.

An under-active seeking system in adulthood could contribute to a person staying stuck in an unloving relationship or a completely soulless, boring job. These people lack that magical drive to transform the seed of disillusionment into a new adventure or an amazing new reality! Maybe this could be a contributing factor to the massive increase in depression rates among within our communities.

Playing verbal games with a child in his or her early years ensures the development of verbal and processing skills around visual and auditory cues. These skills help children learn to read. Such activities also help them to manage their impulses and learn about persistence, winning and losing. Singing and counting games help stimulate young children's brains. These activities develop patterning and sequencing strategies that help with cognitive processing later in life. They are very important in developing the resilience pathways.

Card games, Connect Four, Snakes and Ladders, and Pick-Up-Sticks help children develop hand-eye coordination, memory and concentration. Children also need to understand that it is OK to make mistakes; and parents need to understand that it is OK for their children to make mistakes too and experience disappointment. This is the only way they learn that they can recover from these life realities!

Children need opportunities for creative, exploratory play in stress-free environments, without restrictions on time or freedom. Anecdotal evidence shows that many preschools and primary schools are returning to having longer times for children to play outside in natural environments with dirt, trees, water and grass. Consequently, these schools are noticing an increase in children's creative play, social cohesion, better problem solving, negotiation skills and immersion in the play experience. Children are calmer, happier, less anxious and less stressed. Cognitive learning is still taking place within unstructured play. This type of play is vital for developing social skills like sharing, taking turns, communication skills and dealing with disappointments and delayed gratification.

> Play is the highest expression of human development in childhood, for it alone is the free expression of what is in the child's soul.
>
> *The Education of Man*, Friedrich Froebel (1826).

Physical activity reduces the likelihood of obesity. It is also important for the functioning of the brain as it supports learning and memory through the repair and maintenance of neural circuits. Physical activity can reduce stress and aggression, and it helps regulate mood by increasing the release of serotonin and dopamine, which are essential for emotional and cognitive well-being. Being physically active may be a protective factor against depression. Vigorous play like chasey, jumping on the trampoline or ball games, have another wonderful quality to them other than having fun and getting fit. Physical activity that elevates the heart rate discharges excess energy that builds up from emotional challenges or situations of threat. Even adults feel calmer and more relaxed after physical activity. Exercise releases endorphins and chemicals that promote positive moods and a feeling of well-being. This is another reason why trips to parks, beaches and the bush are so important. They help burn up excess energy, release feel-good hormones and allow everyone to get plenty of fresh air.

Play is the best way to develop a healthy enjoyment of physical activity. That is, the activity is best treated as fun, to help build a positive attitude to physical activity. The family who plays together stays together and they will also be healthier, smarter and less aggressive.

Joseph Chilton Pearce is very concerned that, the child is impelled by millions of years of genetic encoding to interact on a full sensory level with the events of the living world, through which he builds his structures of world knowledge. They must be able to follow this innate coding and drive to connect on a full sensory level with the real world, not a virtual reality world.

Card games, board games and more structured games are valuable for older children and teenagers. It builds on the sense that these older children can play with people they care about, those who are on their inner circle of connectedness. This strengthens their sense of belonging. Games also help children to experience losing, being patient, delaying gratification and taking turns. Being competitive and yet being socially acceptable are vital skills to learn, especially for boys. These are all emotional life skills that will help children and teenagers navigate life better. Thinking skills, communication strategies and creativity is involved when playing many board games. Thinking skills have far-reaching benefits for the developing brain. Research has shown that the brain does not finish its maturing process until around the early twenties. Emotional competence seldom reaches perfection. I know that many parents hate losing at a game of Uno or Snakes and Ladders. Fortunately, the adult pre-frontal lobe allows us to disguise our displeasure a little better—sometimes!

Some of the best play activities can occur from simple things like cardboard boxes, buckets, ice cream containers and empty plastic bottles. What a great way to recycle and provide play opportunities for young children. I can remember the delight a washing machine box gave my sons once. It became a rocket ship, a boat, a tower and a tunnel and the morning they found it soaked through and ruined on the back lawn was a very sad day in the Dent home. Simple bedding sheets make great indoor cubbies for when it's wet outside. Sometimes they can last weeks and you will find very interesting things in them – like vegemite sandwiches with furry green stuff growing all over them when you are finally able to help them dismantle their wonderful creations!

Many excellent books are available for parents and professionals who work with children to provide ideas for interactive play. One I enjoy is, *Creative Play for Your Baby* by Christopher Clouder and Janni Nicol. It has pages of ideas about toys and artistic pursuits to follow at home. These are safe, non-toxic and are guaranteed to be a delight for any young child. Jenny Mosley has many excellent books on traditional games including clapping, skipping and singing games.

Adults who continue to play in their adult life—whether it is organised sport, fishing, golfing, boating or flying kites—are often resilient and able to cope with life's challenges. Having an interest that provides joy is important for maintaining personal well-being. Children tend to model their parents' behaviours, and having parents who enjoy their life through play is one of the best examples to follow.

A final word on play comes from Daniel Goleman, author of, *Emotional Intelligence* and more recently, *Social Intelligence: The New Science of Human Relationships*. Goleman studied the work of Jaak Panksepp.

> The primal subcortical circuitry that prompts the young of all mammals to romp in rough and tumble play seems to have a vital part in the child's neural growth. And the emotional fuel for all that development seems to be delight itself.
>
> Social Intelligence, Daniel Goleman.

This writing validates the common sense notion that children benefit greatly from experiencing sustained moments of joy and delight. It appears that these moments of delight fertilise the growth of circuitry in the amygdala and frontal cortex of the brain. Pankstepp studied the tickling response in mammals, finding that all mammals have 'tickling skin'. In his studies, Pankstepp found that children and other mammals are instinctively drawn to adults who tickle them. Apparently the tickle zone in children runs from the back of the neck and around the rib cage. I am sure many of us remember how hilarious it can be to be tickled by someone safe. The circuitry for playful joy has close ties to the neural networks that make a ticklish child laugh. This means that our brain can become hardwired with an urge to play, one that hurls us into sociability.

Pankstepp argues that many children with hyperactivity, impulsivity and unfocused, rapid shifting from one activity to another (as in ADHD) are in fact seeking the joy and delight response to be activated. He makes a radical, untested proposal to let younger children 'vent' their urge to play in an early-morning free play, rough and tumble recess; then bring them into a classroom after the urge has been sated, when they can more easy pay attention.

Another concern that Pankstepp has with children who receive medications for ADHD, results from his studies on rats. These showed that the psycho-stimulant medications reduced the activity of the brain's play centres—just as they seem to snuff out the playfulness in children. This can be seen to support the premise that children are wired to play, that play should involve fun and delight, and that these states are incredibly helpful for the growing child on many levels. The modern world has complicated the natural patterns of healthy development for many children.

While play may seem like the fun, easy part of being a child, it is also vitally important for building connectedness and brain integration. These vital processes assist with literacy and numeracy; enhance emotional and social awareness; and enhance competence. Play can also build mental well-being and provides the building blocks for being loving, caring human beings who are capable of creating intimate relationships later in life. Let play continue throughout life.

> Ensure that children have lots of fun, plenty of laughter and play. It helps them build physical fitness as well as psychological wellbeing.

The final aspect of play has to do with its healing potential. Children who have been abused or traumatised need play to aid any healing process. In my book play nurtures the mind, the body, the heart and the soul. It strengthens the imagination and allows real children time to be real— to play as children are biologically wired to do. We need to slow our world down to allow children to play more – and know that this is what they need most to grow healthy and happy.

For all the kids who survived the 1930s, 40s, 50s, 60s and 70s

First, we survived being born to mothers who smoked and/or drank while they carried us.

They took aspirin, ate blue cheese dressing, tuna from a can, and didn't get tested for diabetes.

Then after that trauma, our baby cribs were covered with bright coloured lead-based paints.

We had no childproof lids on medicine bottles, doors or cabinets; and when we rode our bikes, we had no helmets, not to mention the risks we took hitchhiking.

As children, we would ride in cars with no seat belts or air bags.

We drank water from the garden hose and not from a bottle.

We shared one soft drink with four friends, from one bottle and no one actually died from this.

We ate white bread and real butter, but we weren't overweight because we were always outside playing.

We would leave home in the morning and play all day, as long as we were back when the streetlights came on.

No one was able to reach us all day. And we were O.K.

We would spend hours building our go-karts out of scraps and then ride down the hill, only to find out we forgot the brakes. After running into the bushes a few times, we learned to solve the problem.

We did not have Playstations, Nintendo's, X-boxes—no video games at all, no 99 channels on cable, no video tape movies, no surround sound, no mobile phones, no ipods, no personal computers, no Internet or Internet chat rooms.

We had friends and we went outside and found them.

We fell out of trees, got cut, broke bones and teeth and there were no lawsuits from these accidents.

We ate worms and mud pies made from dirt, and the worms did not live in us forever.

We were given BB guns [air rifles] for our 10th birthdays, made up games with sticks and tennis balls and although we were told it would happen, we did not put out very many eyes.

We rode bikes or walked to a friend's house and knocked on the door or rang the bell, or just walked in and talked to them.

The idea of a parent bailing us out if we broke the law was unheard of. They actually sided with the law.

This generation has produced some of the best risk-takers, problem solvers and inventors ever.

The past 50 years have been an explosion of innovation and new ideas.

We had freedom, failure, success and responsibility, and we learned how to deal with it all.

(Source: the Internet)

Parent tips for plenty of play

- *Avoid over stimulating young toddlers and children.*
- *Children are biologically wired to learn through play.*
- *Children learn nearly everything through play.*
- *Key social and emotional skills are learned through play.*
- *Play helps children build autonomy and decision making skills.*
- *Play that is unstructured is vitally important in shaping children's innate character and personality.*
- *Avoid play that requires technology and commercialised toys for as long as possible.*
- *Play with your children.*
- *Play helps children learn how to take risks.*
- *Vigorous play diffuses excess emotional energy and calms children down.*
- *The developing cerebellum needs tumbling, rolling, balancing and spinning.*
- *Play that involves the whole family at times is very helpful and healthy.*
- *The more play the better!*

> When imagination and play collide, spontaneously, magic happens for real children.

Children in traditional village type communities are always learning. They learn about the natural world while they play near the women of the tribe. They learn different life skills that help them emotionally and socially while they play with the other children of the tribe. They develop early competence in many areas because the tribe needs its children to help in the primary tasks of gathering food, wood and water, caring for younger children and taking care of the older tribal members. They learn to be responsible in many areas while they are still children.

Building Block 5
Build life skills

The early years are when children begin to build a toolkit of life skills. The more tools in the toolkit, the more resilient the child will be. The first tools in a child's toolkit deal with practical things like being able to dress and feed themselves, going to the toilet unaided, and being able to play with others. All learning is sequential for babies and toddlers and it takes time to become solid memory and repetition of meaningful experiences is the key to building the required neural pathways. The development of these early skills can take lots of patience, time and energy by parents or carers. Many early years teachers are concerned that more children are coming to preschool and kindergarten without having mastered toilet training skills. Child care workers also express concern that parents are expecting them to take the responsibility of toilet training their young children during the day. These same parents are happy to leave a nappy on once they collect their children at the end of the day.

> All children learn, grow and master life skills at differing rates. There is no competition in raising children—there never has been and never should be.

Building up the life skills toolkit starts from birth, and sometimes it is the little things, like getting a drink of water for themselves when they need to, are the big things. These small milestones build a child's belief in their competence to accomplish tasks, which in turn helps build their self esteem. Adults should avoid the one or two word commands and rather converse with their toddlers and young children about things like:

- "To be safe we hold hands when we cross busy roads....."

- "Why do we wash our hands after going to the toilet?"

- "Why are vegetables good for us?"

- "What does sour taste like?"

- "Sleep makes our brains and our bodies healthy and smart – so let's get to sleep!"

- "What are seat belts used for?"

- "How do you know when you are thirsty or hungry?"

- "You seem angry that Sam has taken your toy from you – how else can you show your anger without biting Sam?"

- "Shall we clean up all these toys before we have lunch, or shall we do it after we have lunch?"

Conversational language and more coherent speaking opportunities are now seen to be equally important as being read to in the first three years of life for building the pathways to literacy. These allow children to explore conversation and the hidden patterns within the spoken language. They also give children a sense of being noticed and having value. As a result, children are strongly supported in the life skill of 'having a voice' and of being heard—attributes expressed by assertive and resilient people. Anyone who feels unheard often struggles with their self esteem and they can feel isolated, unaccepted or unvalued. They may give up more easily with other challenges that come their way and feel disillusioned with the world in other ways. This can influence their emotional and social intelligence developing in an optimal way.

Healthy communication is a life skill adults keep working on throughout life. I found the book by Naomi Aldort, *Raising Our Children, Raising Ourselves* refreshingly original in the way she explored communicating honestly with our children. Some parents achieve this form of responsible communicating quite naturally and may not even be aware that they do it. Naomi uses the acronym SALVE to explain how her model works. The key step is the first where you separate yourself from your child's behaviour and emotions with some silent self-talk. This technique is a good way of becoming aware of the voice of the inner critic in our own head—the critical parent voice that runs automatically.

The next step is the 'A', which is paying full *attention* to your child. Then the 'L' is *listening* to what his or her words or actions may be saying. The 'V' is where we *validate* their feelings and their needs without judgement. The final 'E' is about *empowering* the child to resolve their own upset and by trusting that they can. This simple process is the best I have ever come across for parenting with conscious awareness. I find that the hardest step is the first step, to really pause before reacting with your own inner critical parent. The same goes for asking children to meet one of your needs, like picking up their wet towel. So often we command, which immediately smells of disrespect. A great clue offered by Naomi is **to ask your children in the same way you would ask an adult friend.**

Another valuable message I received from Naomi's book was how to express regret so that a child feels healed. Instead of saying "I am sorry I hurt you," which means we take responsibility for the child's choice of emotion, we can say, "I yelled at you; I wish I hadn't and I am sorry". We need to avoid taking responsibility for our children's feelings because it invalidates those feelings. We choose our own feelings, no one can make us feel anything unless we choose to feel it! This is an excellent life skill that builds emotional competence.

Essential life skills involve using manners, etiquette, road rules, practising good hygiene—such as bathing and cleaning teeth, doing up buttons and tying shoelaces. These are the little things that other children may use to tease another child. Parents must be proactive to help their children gain essential life skills so the children are able to take care of their own age-appropriate needs – and not expect child care, kindergarten or pre school to be places where children learn these vital life skills. Children can be bullied and teased if they are unable to complete basic tasks when at preschool. This can be very painful and may leave scars that later impact on his or her ability to be resilient. Peer-based sanctions and observations can, however, serve as great motivators as well. Children who notice they are the only ones in a class who cannot tie up their shoelaces are suddenly very keen to learn this skill—one of my sons mastered it overnight when he was in Grade one. I had failed him by using elastic sided boots instead of lace-up shoes—too many busy lads to keep in lace-up shoes in my house!

Much of the essential learning that takes place in childhood, especially in the early years, is building emotional and social competence. We now know there are many ways of being intelligent and one of these is emotional intelligence (EQ). Research shows that 80% of a person's potential to be successful in life has to do with their EQ and not their IQ (Daniel Goleman). We can encourage emotional intelligence and competence from an early age because this builds resilience for later in life.

Qualities of emotional intelligence

- Awareness of feeling states.
- Being able to motivate oneself.
- Persistence in the face of frustration.
- Impulse control.
- Delayed gratification.
- Regulation of one's moods.
- Keeping distress from swamping one's ability to think.
- Ability to accurately empathise.
- Hopefulness.

Emotional Intelligence, Daniel Goleman. ,1995

The main pathways that allow us to understand and manage our emotions are created in early childhood. Anne Manne in her book, *Motherhood: How Should We Care for Our Children* writes that we now understand that children can suffer from post-traumatic stress disorder or have long term damage from a single episode of terrible trauma. This can happen without any outward signs and the child may appear unharmed. Babies and children who are 'frozen out', or who experience rejection, whether it is physically, emotionally or verbally, are at great risk of struggling socially and emotionally for the rest of their lives. Their inability to be empathetic or to form caring loving relationships is seriously and often permanently impaired. This lack of emotional skills in their kit bag can increase the chances of them making very poor decisions in life. This lack can cause enormous suffering, especially around violent behaviour, criminality, addictive patterns and abuse.

> Abused and neglected children have extremely high rates of disorganised and disorientated attachments which is highly correlated with the development of personality disorders.
>
> *Motherhood*, Anne Manne (2005).

The critical time for young children to develop the ability to be empathetic, gentle and kind is under four years of age. If a very young child is given the opportunity to interact with a small kitten or puppy with adult guidance, he or she can learn what being gentle and caring means. I have seen many toddlers who have nearly squeezed the life out of a kitten before they learned what gentle really meant! Children without this opportunity may be unable to care that they are being rough or hurting others. This inability to feel empathy is a significant behavioural deprivation and could mean that an individual may have difficulty in relationships, especially when it comes to intimacy. There is one other window when the brain can build pathways that support empathetic behaviour, and that is between approximately 13–15 years of age, when the brain has a massive growth spurt. This can be an excellent time to get a small pet as your teenager can still learn how to be gentle and caring in this window. Some researchers argue that if this vital emotional development does not happen by the time a person is 15 or 16 years of age then it will be very difficult for them to develop it—ever. This lack of empathy is a key aspect that is evident in teenagers and adults who were ignored as children and who experienced very little play. Such is the essential nature of much of the emotional and social learning that many of today's adults ignore or invalidate in favour of smart cognitive and physical development.

Many children who behave as bullies have problems with empathy. This emotional competency is only learned through life experience and the guidance of a caring adult. Tim Gill in his book, *No Risk* writes about his concerns that the modern world has developed a growing overreaction to minor problems in childhood. Play fighting, rough and tumble and even combative role-play are very normal parts of childhood. Yet in today's world these forms of play are often misinterpreted as forms of bullying, or a precursor to bullying, and are banned. Early years researcher, Penny Holland in her book, *We Don't Play With Guns* argues that these forms of play are outward signs of a sophisticated and largely unconscious learning process that helps to build emotional and social life skills. Children learn how to read key facial expressions and body language, and can quite clearly tell the difference between play and the real thing.

Despite research findings, play fighting has come to be seen as a disturbing facet of childhood and one which children need to be saved (Tim Gill). This shift in parenting could be contributing to boys being unable to negotiate tricky social situations later in life and where they get into serious trouble by misreading the social cues between play and a real threat. Children need to learn the many invisible codes of behaviour that provide life skills. This learning is being eroded by the current attitude towards demonising normal childhood misbehaviour—children are meant to make mistakes with the choices they make because they are children.

Bullying has become such a hot topic in schools that it too may have contaminated some of today's key life skill development for children. The original definition of bullying was that it involved sustained, repeated maltreatment based on a power imbalance between victim and perpetrator (Tim Gill). In recent bullying definitions it has been softened to include any form of victimisation or harassment perpetrated by another child or young person (*Dangerous People, Dangerous Places: The Nature and Location of Young People's Victimisation and Fear*, J. Deakin, 2006). This is of great concern as children are still developing skills to be assertive and they will make mistakes at times. Such an over-reaction encourages adults to feel under pressure to take every misdemeanour seriously and to step in and work out conflicts—we may be interrupting a normal part of social and emotional development. We need to be careful that the over-parenting pressures of today's modern world are not diluting the value of everyday unpleasantness, and of children learning for themselves how to deal with it. Wrapping our children in cotton wool can weaken their resilience later in life. At the same time, we must protect and act when real bullying occurs. At other times we need to learn to step back and let kids be kids when other social challenges occur. Vital emotional learning can be taking place.

Coping with significant loss and death is another vital life skill that children can benefit from experiencing while still children. A young child's pet dying introduces the life challenge of loss. The child is able to explore death and to learn that grief creates emotional pain that eventually fades and goes away. They learn about the need to dispose of the deceased's body reverently and that some things bring comfort, like ceremony, prayers or leaving flowers at the grave. This builds a template for future death experiences and builds resilience and the ability to recover, which are needed later in life if and when they experience a major loss.

I have a strong belief that children under 10 years of age benefit from being supported in the belief that when we die a special part of us continues on to a beautiful place. Those who have a faith already share this information with their children. However, those without a faith may create a potential emotional challenge for their children that can cause deep emotional distress if ever they experience a sudden death. My explanation is that the imagination protects and insulates children from the pain and challenges of the adult world. If they can imagine that this wonderful place exists then it brings them enormous comfort if a death occurs. They will say things like, "Nanny must be with Spotty now Mummy."; or "I hope they still have chocolate and ice cream in heaven because Poppy loved them!" Those who have no belief in the continuation of the soul or human spirit or essence of a loved one can be reassured that when your child gets to be older, they can discover their own spiritual pathway. It's much like discovering that maybe Santa is not a real being; it will never take away the positive spirit of the time of Christmas. There comes a time when the magical time of childhood is tainted by reality, however it supports young children during a vital stage of their lives.

If you would like to learn more about children and how they process death, please feel free to use the link below. It is for an article I wrote for the *Kindred Parenting* magazine in March 2008 called, *Death Through the Eyes of a Child*. You have my permission to print it and use it as a reference, or to share it with others.
www.maggiedent.com/Death_through_eyes_of_child.pdf

Anecdotal evidence suggests that early years teachers are noticing more children with emotional incompetence. An increased amount of time in front of screens instead of playing in real environments may be a contributing factor. Interaction with others helps strengthen children's emotional literacy and helps them to understand others and themselves. But this does not develop well if there is an over-reliance on the virtual world of television or computers. Teachers are finding that some children have poor impulse control and an inability to persist at challenging tasks. Reluctance or refusal to keep trying can impact enormously both in the school environment and later in life. Persistence is another emotional competency that is being eroded by the pressures of modern life, especially with our hurry-up, in an instant focus.

> Children need to be allowed to have a childhood, without the pressures of performing, conforming and being scheduled into a life filled with inappropriate expectations. Our challenge is not to become caught up in a rushed and hurried world and certainly not to allow our children to be swept along its manic course.
>
> Kathy Walker.

Even though play has been covered in the previous building block, it is important to affirm how valuable play is in learning key life skills. We know that play allows children to take risks, make mistakes, learn to wait, solve problems and—very importantly—to learn to win and lose graciously. Losing can hurt and makes us feel awful, however we do recover. One of my sons was a passionate soccer player in his boyhood. He was devastated when his soccer team lost a grand final because he missed a penalty shot. He cried for quite a time and was inconsolable. It is helpful to leave a child for a short time to really experience the pain of losing before rushing in to comfort. This is how children learn that they can overcome massive disappointment and a deep sense of loss. When you do offer reassurance, avoid using treats or sweets, you could be setting up a lifetime pattern of comfort that can be detrimental. Nothing beats hugs, warm safe touch and encouraging words of reassurance that validate those irrational feelings that swamp us at such times. When all else fails there is always tickling on the upper back......

Play in the natural world is especially beneficial for children when in the company of children of differing ages. This is how children learn to make choices, take risks and become responsible for younger children. Play with other children is vital to teach how to be a social being, make and keep friends, and experience the wonder of absorbed play. Interactive play with other children has benefits that are emotional, social, cognitive and spiritual. The two main things to remember about play are:
1. The more the better.
2. The more child-centred the better.

There was once a large bush area at a primary school in a country town where children had to be over eight years of age to play in. This area had fallen logs, shrubs and rocks and was supervised quite loosely in order for the students to play games that could go on for days or even weeks. The boys were especially fond of this area. It was profoundly important in the growth and development of the students because they were able to continue games that evolved over time—a fabulous opportunity for social learning and creative thinking opportunities. Unfortunately, like with many other modern decisions the area has been cleared and the students have only the oval and basketball courts to play on.

Social awareness has a huge impact on our resilience and is a life skill that takes time to develop—we continue to work on it as adults. Relationships are essential in terms of strengthening resilience when things get tough. We only turn to those with whom we have been able to develop authentic, emotionally honest relationships. Loneliness and isolation are serious diseases of the mind, body and soul that can be factors contributing to mental illness, homelessness, alienation and life disasters. It is always a reminder during times of trauma and tragedy that the only things that really matter are simply those who come home to us, those whom we love the most— not our jobs, house or car. Building connectedness is an essential part of the protective factors involved in being resilient.

In global resilience studies having a sense of humour is recognised as being a very valuable life skill. It is a huge protective factor in school yards where it can protect children from unwanted harassment or bullying. There are so many benefits that can be gained on many levels from laughter.

Laughter:

- transforms emotional states
- stimulates endorphins and creates well being
- increases levels of serotonin
- is a key coping skill, especially for boys
- is an anti-bullying strategy
- encourages lightening up for serious moments

- is a bonding experience when shared in groups
- builds inclusivity and connectedness
- releases tension and stress
- is a key element in effective communication, especially in close relationships
- is an antidote to violence.

Laughter can transform negative emotional states faster than almost any other strategy or technique a parent can use. It is unfortunate that a sense of humour does not arrive in a box underneath the Christmas tree; it would be so much easier than cultivating it as a child has to do, along with so many life skills. There are times when young children use inappropriate humour in certain circumstances. Risqué or 'shed' humour has a very important place in the Australian psychology and larrikin humour helps to negate our depreciatory humour and language patterns. Culturally we tend to 'put things down' or deflate compliments, "Wow, you have scrubbed up pretty good tonight darling!" can be an Australian compliment that is genuinely meant to be kind. An overt compliment like, "Wow, you look beautiful tonight!" could get you a quick kick in the knee! This cultural nuance needs humour and without it people can easily take offence. Apprentice tradesmen are sometimes the brunt of antics and pranks by older staff. Some young lads are asked to find the left-handed screwdriver or the striped paint. When people realise it has been a joke, those with a sense of humour are able to laugh about it rather than feel shame and deep embarrassment.

Sharing simple riddles and jokes with young children is an excellent way to nurture a sense of humour. There will be times when the children share a joke that is a little inappropriate and it's important to avoid shaming or overtly sanctioning their attempts. One of my sons—who was in Year one at the time—came home busting to tell a joke at the dinner table. It went like this:

"Mummy what's the difference between a light bulb and a pregnant lady?" The answer was, "Well, you can un-screw the light bulb!"

Needless to say his older brothers loved the joke and he had no idea what the joke was about. He was just passing on something he had heard at school.

One way to encourage laughter and lightness in the home is to have funny books and riddle books beside the toilet. This is a place that everyone has to visit and having some material that builds a sense of humour is making very valuable use of this little room. I particularly enjoy, *366 Fun Quotes and Observations of Life* books by David Koutsoukis. These books combine humour with interesting fun facts and can be educational as well as entertaining. A few of my favourite lines from this book are:
"No man has ever been shot while doing the dishes."
"Five out of four people have trouble with fractions."
"If one synchronised swimmer drowns does that mean all the others have to?"
"What happens if you get scared half to death twice?"
"Marriage is the chief cause of divorce."
"Be careful not to be too open minded—your brains might fall out."

By reading these books and sharing the funny bits with family, children can learn the nuances of joke telling and of being humorous. This is a very important part of communication among friends and family. Only practise can improve anyone's ability to be humorous. I can still remember wondering what was wrong with me during my teenage years because I didn't seem to be able to 'get' jokes; I just missed what was funny. I still remember feeling quite stupid as well.

The capacity to laugh deeply and in an uninhibited way is another life skill that takes developing. Children who feel safe and valued can even fall over when they get an attack of giggles or laughter. A positive gauge of the well being of a child can be how often they smile and laugh. It is something that is very difficult to fake as children—if they are unhappy or frightened their face shows it. As adults we need to treasure these exquisite moments of joy.

> Humour also assists in accepting life's imperfections, inevitabilities, difficulties, frustrations and disappointments. It helps us to realise what we cannot control, such as death, the behaviour of other people, incompetence, ageing, physical limitations and illness. Jokes and funny throw away lines can also communicate messages that help us understand what is normal and typical. In knowing that others share some of the same feelings, perceptions and troubles, we feel more empowered to deal with these troubles.
>
> *Bounce Back! Teacher's Handbook*,
> Helen McGrath and Toni Noble (2006–2007).

Laughter and lightness in homes and classrooms shows safety and connectedness. We now have laughter therapy groups that help people to laugh again; such is the healing potential of triggering those positive brain chemicals.

On the first day of school, a first-grader handed his teacher a note from his mother. The note read, "The opinions expressed by this child are not necessarily those of his parents".

I recommend that parents use props and puppets to increase the levels of lightness in the house. Witch's hats can warn children that mum is feeling grumpy and her tiara will help children know she's feeling happy. Puppets can cheer up any place, they become a metaphor that can communicate so powerfully. I know teachers who have the clean-up puppet, the quiet time mouse, the Tigger puppet for exercise time and the serious owl for proper chats about values. Be adventuresome and lighten up, your children will come with you. In the process you too could make your spirit and heart happier, and help your stress levels dissolve away.

Children who are encouraged to think for themselves are given valuable cognitive processing skills for their whole life. Flexible thinking is definitely a protective factor when adversity hits.

> It is thinking style that determines resilience–more than genetics, more than intelligence, more than any other single factor.
>
> *The Resilience Factor*, K. Reivich and A. Shatte (2002).

An important life skill involves the art of finding solutions. This involves helping children to discover other choices that they could make in response to a challenge, whether a disagreement with a friend or a toy that has broken.

A commitment to search for solutions begins with the adult. Before you fix a problem for a child, help them to explore ways to overcome it him or herself. Children do not yet have a frontal lobe in their brains where reasoning and problem solving takes place but they can develop thinking skills that empower them to manage some situations themselves. There is a great temptation for parents to rescue their children from struggles and challenges however this denies them vital opportunities to learn life management skills for themselves.

One of Edward de Bono's early books called "Children Solve Problems" showed how children were capable of the most amazing, innovative problem solving when left to their own devices. One of the tasks he set involved coming up with a solution to stop cats and dogs fighting – the varied responses were ingenious. If encouraged to think, children are very capable and inventive. The key is giving them the opportunity while they are young, so that it becomes 'normal' behaviour for them.

As adults we must be careful to appreciate that they do see the world through the eyes of a child. So their way of interpreting things and events is quite different from ours. Being empathetic and really listening to what children are telling us are vital in helping them to develop the thinking strategies needed to review and explore what's happening.

When adults:	The child feels:
Threaten	"I don't count."
Command	"I'm bad."
Preach	"you don't like me."
Lecture	"I can't do anything right."

If we want to raise resilient children, our words and actions must convey to them that none of their questions are silly or irrelevant.

Nurturing Resilience in Our Children, Robert Brooks and Sam Goldstein (2002).

Some sentence beginnings that may help encourage thinking and cognitive processing in children include:

- *"How might we resolve this?"*
- *"How can we make this better?"*
- *"What do you think needs to happen now?"*
- *"What questions do you have about what we have just done?"*
- *"What can I do to help you complete this task?"*
- *"Sounds like you/we have a problem."*
- *"Whose problem is this?"*
- *"How can we work together to get the best outcome here?"*
- *"There is a conflict here. How can I help you to sort it out?"*
- *"Please make a decision to stay with us or go to a place where you can clam down." CHOOSE. DECIDE. PICK.*
- *"Please consider making a different choice."*
- *"Act as if you have already done this..."*
- *"Check yourself. Do you have everything to do this?"*

- *"Check it out inside. Does it feel right?"*
- *"What's your goal? What's your intention?"*
- *"What do you attribute that to? How did you produce that result?"*
- *"I'm willing to help you complete this task."*
- *"I know you can handle it!"*
- *"What do you think we can do now?"*
- *"It won't be long before you will be able to do this."*
- *"Every problem has a solution."*
- *"I noticed that..."*
- *"Different people have different needs." (In response to, "It's not fair!")*
- *"Inch by inch we can achieve things..."*
- *"Now that's interesting!"*

Children who are surrounded by optimistic language, language that encourages thinking and decision making, have the opportunities become resilient when managing setbacks and challenges. They are much less likely to succumb to 'learned helplessness', where they expect adults to always be there to do things for them. There is a line between doing too much for your children and having expectations that are too high, and possibly inappropriate, for your children. Parents need to be careful.

> Inappropriate expectations of the child's stage and age development, along with a belief that learning appropriate behaviours is all about "training" are the pitfalls (some) parents are likely to fall into.
>
> Kathy Walker.

Flexible and creative thinking are beneficial in developing real resilience. Children are not little adults. They grow according to their brain and gross motor skill development. They model themselves on significant adults in their lives and are constantly picking up cues from conversations on thinking patterns. Children's thinking skills can be positively influenced by positive adults, and negatively influenced by depressive or aggressive adults.

We continue to face an uncertain future with depleting oil supplies and the effects of global warming. It is more important than ever that we prepare our children by helping them to develop life skills that build on environmental appreciation and ecological sustainability. The return of home vegetable gardens is a great place to start. Children love to be involved anywhere there is dirt; and watching seeds turn into shoots and seedlings is quite magical for small children. If space is limited then even pots with fresh herbs are a great experience for children; and to pick fresh herbs and take them into the kitchen can provide an important life awareness to take into adulthood. There are children who have no idea where milk comes from, or even what many fruit and vegetables are. Gardening is a great way to be alongside your children as they play, and it helps ground us and slow us down as well. This outside activity can also help children develop an understanding of the seasons and the amazing flow of natural life. These may seem small things to adults, however they are big for children. Outside activities can also plant a seed of possibility for a child, which may develop into a potential career path later in life. I know of zoologists who have grown from being frog gatherers and lizard catchers as children. Steve Irwin's passion for wildlife would have started early in his childhood as he followed his father's love of the natural world. I wonder what creatures were hiding in his bedroom at times!

Strong community support is a fundamental part of many cultures today. All families and friends take responsibility for ensuring everyone gains the necessary social and life skills so they are valued and able to contribute to the well-being of the whole community. In these communities people see their role in helping to raise children as an honour and privilege. The art of cooperatively co-parenting children ensures children have the best opportunity to learn as many life skills as possible while they are young.

Anthropologists have known for some time that children who are raised in communal parenting groups fare much better. In the nineteenth century—a time of huge child abandonment rates all over Europe—the island of Sardinia enjoyed one of the best infant survival rates, despite being one of the poorest economies. Unlike most European mothers, Sardinian women joined together in supportive, cooperative mothering groups. Mothers who don't parent alone tend to be much happier (*Heart to Heart Parenting*, Robin Grille, 2008).

Life skills are something that we continue to gather as we continue through life. We need to be realistic with what we expect children to be able to do and ask only for age appropriate skills. Even at 35 years if age I have almost been hit by a car when crossing a road because I was not paying attention. Now with menopause I seem to have lost a few of my life skills completely! The good thing is that I seem to have forgotten what those life skills were anyway!

Parent Tips for Building Life Skills

- *Invest energy throughout your child's early years to help them build basic life skills like dressing themselves, cleaning teeth, toileting, getting own drinks and light snacks, washing hands after going to toilet, tying shoelaces.*

- *Engage in simple conversations with your children often—avoid talking at them.*
- *Remember that children have to do things many times before the neural pathway is established for learning to occur.*
- *Connectedness helps build social and emotional comfort and competence.*
- *Ensure that you meaningfully engage with each of your children, especially through repeated play and games—including rough and tumble.*
- *Allow children to experience failure and disappointment before offering comfort.*
- *Try to get pets that have a habit of dying, like guinea pigs, mice and goldfish so children can experience death and loss.*
- *A sense of humour needs to be developed over time. Help your children to learn what is appropriate humour.*
- *Be careful to avoid confusing bullying with normal unpleasant events of childhood.*
- *Whole communities help children build life skills— everyone can help.*
- *Childhood is a time of constant learning. Be careful not to shame a child because he or she is unable to master a life skill.*
- *Avoid comparing siblings and never assume a child knows how to do something you think they should know.*
- *Encourage thinking skills from a young age.*
- *Avoid rescuing your children and be careful about doing too much for them.*

One of the most significant benefits of raising children within a tribal community was that there were many people who were positively involved in children's lives. This created a deep sense of belonging and solidarity for the children of the tribe. Rituals and shared activities strengthened the bonds of affection and connectedness. Time spent playing or being involved with children was seen as important because the tribe's future was seen to be in their hands. The greater good of the whole tribe was always the main driving focus and this meant that people of every age were valued and appreciated. It still takes many caring people to raise one healthy, happy child.

Building Block 6
Meaningful involvement with positive adults

Being surrounded by safe, caring people helps children to build positive expectations about their world. And it is the secret ingredient of the 'meaningful involvement' building block that builds the pathways to personal acceptance and connectedness.

> Our effectiveness as parents will be in direct proportion to the strength of the connection we have with our child.
>
> Pam Leo.

Children are constantly forming perceptions or core concepts that become their unconscious beliefs. These deep-seated beliefs become the guiding mental templates from which the child interprets the world. If a child is ignored or treated with critical words, he or she is likely to create core beliefs of being 'useless', 'unlovable' or 'not enough'. For example, children who struggle with reading in Grade one at school may believe that they are dumb and stupid. Readiness to read may occur any time between 4–14 years of age, yet these children's belief systems unjustly inhibit them from learning to read. Positive expectations from adults can help a child avoid setting up a negative, self-fulfilling prophecy towards their schooling and all learning.

> What began as a pattern of interaction in relationships
> becomes generalised into expectations of the world, coded
> unconsciously, part of the structure of the mind. It becomes a
> kind of internal map of the self, of the other, of self with other.
>
> Anne Manne.

Children are constantly forming core concepts from their
immediate environment and the emotionally significant events
that happen in their lives. Feeling disconnected, unloved and
unwanted are challenging negative beliefs to change and can
have a large impact for life. This is why meaningful involvement
with their primary caregivers is a vital stage of early development.
This does not just mean that the child knows his or her main
caregivers, it means that those primary caregivers have formed a
bond of attachment and affection with the child. Together they
create a relationship that is based on trust and genuine positive
regard. This is why parents need to be careful of who they allow
to care for their children.

> Most core beliefs are formed before children are 7 years of age
> and shape the way that they see the world. Research suggests
> that negative thought patterns in childhood last for life and can
> contribute to mental ill health in adulthood, as well as
> preventing the full realisation of one's potential
>
> *Raising Resilient Children*, R. Brooks and S. Goldstein (2001).

If there is not a clear bond of trust and care, and young children
will show clearly if that is so when you mention the carer's name
or by their behaviour when they see that carer, then think
carefully about entrusting your child to that person or centre.

> There is all the difference in the world between leaving your child with an unfamiliar person and leaving her with her grieving for her "gone Mummy" in the care of a clam, warm, loving person with whom she feels safe. If there are no loving arms you are risking the activation of high levels of stress hormones in your child's brain.
>
> Margot Sunderland.

The separation distress mechanism in the lower brain is genetically wired to be hypersensitive. In the early days of mankind a baby was at great risk if it was separated from its mother; this mechanism ensured that the baby became loudly distressed and so could be found more easily. We must remember that separation hurts babies, much like physical pain. The sensitive early years are a key time for developing core beliefs about trust and safety. Children can be left with other primary carers without any harm, provided the bond of affection is present. The same goes for extended family. If a grandmother dislikes young children and is distant and aloof to them, you could easily be damaging the development of the children's self concepts that they take with them throughout life.

Janet Gongaleze-Mena in the book, *Infants, Toddlers and Caregivers* writes that the caregiver understands how important it is to respect even the youngest infant. She always talks to babies to prepare them for what will happen in fact she never does anything to them without telling them first. She always thinks of them as people....the ultimate is to communicate without words. That means that you're very close to someone when you can do that.

This approach demonstrates the definition of respectful responsive and reciprocal care. These repeated interactions show the infant that he or she is a worthwhile person and are vital to healthy development on all levels.

Adults can help children develop positive thought patterns and core beliefs by expressing optimistic language, avoiding shaming and blame-based language. For example, if a child spills a drink a parent could say:

> *"Never mind accidents happen, let's clean it up together."*

Or, they could say:

> *"How stupid you are! Why don't you watch what you are doing next time!"*

Meaningful involvement can be confused with quality time with a child. Meaningful involvement is an emotional and spiritual connection that can be demonstrated even from a distance. Fathers are vitally important in this circle of love and it is very heartening to see the father's movement gaining credibility and synergy in Australia today. An aunty who has a deep connection to a child can show that bond even when she is living a long way from where the child lives, by staying in touch by phone. She can call and chat about little things as well as the big things, like concerts and other social markers. She may send postcards when she goes on holidays and have a special name she calls the child that is just between the two of them. She would know the child's favourite colour, food and picture books. If the child has a special interest in frogs or bears she would keep an eye out for articles or posters that she can get for him or her. The aunty comes to most if not all birthdays and shares in Christmas and Easter family gatherings. This is what meaningful involvement is for a child. The depth of involvement is essential for well being on many levels, especially in later childhood and adolescence. Parents, biological family, non-biological family, child care workers, nannies and even caring neighbours can all fill this need within children. There is only one thing for sure—the more the better, the deeper the connection the better.

I have a couple of very special young children who I love and have a special bond with—I am still waiting for biological grandchildren! Firstly, I feel blessed that I am able to share these children's beautiful lives. Secondly, the bond does not take a lot of work to keep strong. I chat to them when I call to speak to their parents; I know what makes them laugh and what things they value in their lives. When I visit, I am prepared to be dragged away from the adults to play one on one because I know we have little time to do that and we both love the experience. Children know when people have an open and loving heart, and the more people they meet in their lives who are like this the more they will anticipate finding such people as they grow up.

In a research study done in 1998 by psychologist Raymond Starr of the University of Maryland, he found that abused and neglected children can escape the cycle of becoming abusive parents if they had one nurturing adult as their mentor to support them emotionally and psychologically. We can all make a difference in the lives of disadvantaged children. We simply have to have the courage to care and really connect.

Within our family we have a very special, adopted grandmother called Pat. She looked after my lads one night when I was a solo Mum and arrived laden with food and chocolates—needless to say she was most welcome. On a future dinner visit the youngest of the boys asked if she would be their grandma because she was really nice. Since then Pat has been driving miles to come to each of the boys significant events, like 21st birthdays, and will always be a valued and special part of our extended family.

> A condition called learned helplessness does exist. This occurs when a child, often with special needs, receives special care and assistance. After a time they become dependent and anticipate help, they learn to become helpless. This can happen with over-protective parenting as well.
>
> K. Reivich and A. Shatte.

Not only do primary carers need to be careful of 'learned helplessness' they also need to be mindful of suppression and indulgence. These can occur when we become overwhelmed or exhausted, causing us to respond in a reactive way to our children's demands. Imagine an unhappy child at the checkout who is demanding a sweet. If your love-cup for your child is low, you may say,

"Don't be so silly! You don't deserve anything because you have been awful this morning. You are very naughty!" (suppression)

Or you may say,
"Here have it and shut up! Anything for peace!" (indulgence)

Children only learn life skills by carrying them out often. This is important for building resilient life patterns that help us overcome challenges and adversity. Adults who have a meaningful involvement with children can support their skill building; it takes extra care and attention for some children and more than parent help is needed.

We have a very special young man in our family's life; he is called Jarvis and has autism. We moved to the other side of Australia and yet continue to be a valued part of his life. He is now speaking and the other night when my husband Steve called to say 'Hi', Jarvis answered the phone. This was not a first, however the fact that he spoke on the phone was a real first! He kept saying "Maggie, Maggie" and it brought tears to both our eyes. His mum, dad and sister Aslin are part of our circle of 'inner circles of affection'. Meaningful involvement is a fabulous two-way street—both sides benefit.

Research supports the idea of not hurrying early independence in young children, especially if it is for the convenience of the adults. A clingy, insecure baby needs to be reassured for as long as it takes for him or her to grow into a place of new emotional strength. These babies and infants can be hard work and that's another reason why having others involved in your life can be so important when you are parents. Don't be afraid to ask someone in your community, someone who you feel is kind and caring. There are many retired men and women who may love to become involved, it just takes the courage to ask.

School volunteers are another source of wonderful meaningful involvement, especially if it can evolve over a few years. This initiative from Western Australia has now been introduced to other Australian states. This mentor relationship has been shown to really make a difference in the lives of children socially, emotionally and cognitively; and the volunteers are winners as well. It simply affirms that it takes a whole village to raise a child. If you are interested in learning how to take part in this excellent initiative explore their web site at www.svp.org.au.

The art of 'being present' with a child is an essential building block for a healthy self esteem. This means being focused on the child and the activity; and not thinking of other things or partially viewing the television. Young children can often detect when you are not being honest energetically.

> When a child feels safe to express himself, when he has power to steer his life, and he is secure in knowing that his needs are taken care of, he can experience himself as worthy and loved.
>
> *Raising Our Children, Raising Ourselves*, Naomi Aldort (2006).

How many opportunities are we offering our children so that they can be creative, original and as expressive as they wish? The following list of possibilities has perfect ways for you to be meaningfully involved with your child.

- *Are you comfortable with dirt, mud, paint, water and glue?*
- *Do you have an area around your home where your child can get 'down-and-dirty' with their creativity?*
- *Do you have a strategy that helps your child keep his or her creative mess outside, like a cleaning bucket or bowl and towel?*
- *Do you join in with your child when invited?*
- *Do you keep the 'creation' as your child leaves it or do you quickly clean it away, as soon as possible?*
- *When did your child last make a cubby—inside or outside the house?*
- *Have you brought home any big boxes lately for your child to play with?*

- *When did you last watch ants or butterflies with your child?*
- *If your child likes music is it all on CD or do you allow them to make their own sounds and rhythms on pots and pans?*
- *Do you have TV-free days?*
- *How many sand castles and sculptures have you made?*
- *How many mud pies have you cooked?*
- *How many dozen pipe cleaners or pop sticks have you bought?*
- *How many sidewalk chalk packs have you been through?*
- *What does the outside of your fridge look like?*
- *Have you ever made capes for your child to wear?*
- *Have you hand-painted kids t-shirts with them?*
- *How many framed 'kid's bits' do you have?*
- *How many homemade kites have you made and flown?*
- *When did you last have races with leaf or bark boats?*
- *When did you last make fresh play dough?*
- *When did you last have fresh sand in the sand pit?*
- *How often have you danced with your child?*
- *Have you made cookies using shape cutters with your child?*
- *Have you made homemade chocolates in moulds?*
- *When did you last have a treasure hunt in the garden or park?*
- *When did you last play hide and seek with your child?*
- *Have you kept kisses or wishes in a jar?*
- *Has your child grown anything from seed?*
- *When did you take your child to the library to pick out story and picture books they wanted?*
- *Do you have a box of dress-up clothes?*
- *When did you take your child camping away from the technological world and into the natural world?*

People who are connected to children can also offer some of these possibilities to help tired or busy parents. Respite really helps parents, especially those with challenging, highly spirited children or children with special needs. I have an American friend who always carries small bottles of bubbles for blowing in her handbag for whenever she meets children on her travels. She has made so many special connections with children in trains, planes and shopping centres that she could write a book about it.

The meaningfully involved circle of adults in your children's life may benefit from knowing the following three reasons for unacceptable behaviour in children:

1.   *The child is experiencing a need. Unrecognised and unmet needs can cause children to act badly. The needs can be food, sleep, thirst, touch, affection, recognition or acceptance. The unmet need is often linked to the perception of a lack of love.*
2.   *The child has insufficient information to make a better decision. Be mindful of misinformation or misinterpretation. Always remember that children are interpreting the world all the time through their eyes, not an adult's.*
3.   *The child is harbouring painful, pent-up feelings that need to be expressed in a harmless way. This is what we call emotional discharge or diffusing.*

Alentha Solter, PhD

These three points are very helpful when seeking reasons for why children make inappropriate responses to their environment. Always remember, they are children. Even as older children they can still respond in ways that challenge you, and even as teenagers they make poor choices. As adults we do the same, just less often!

> Children often feel helpless because they are small and inexperienced in a complex, big and fast world – so many machines they can't touch, big people and animals they may fear, places they can't go on their own, heights they cannot reach, things they need help with, events they find scary and speeds they cannot grasps. Many of their upsets result from feeling helpless.
>
> Naomi Aldort.

We do have more knowledge than ever before, and with more conscious and aware parenting, today's children in the Western world should be in great shape. However, they appear to be fatter, sadder, sicker and more disconnected than in previous generations. From my viewpoint, a key factor is that knowledge without conscious action is a toothless tiger. The pressures of modern living with the massive consumerism, media distortions and rapid way of life have meant that our world has become more materialistic and self focused. Our traditional communities were driven by the greater good; and the circles of care ensured that everyone was cared for, the young, old, sick—everyone, without prejudice.

This ancient pattern of solidarity and collective responsibility ensured not only the continuation of the community but also the preservation of the physical world for future generations. Every child was seen as a gift and a miracle from Mother Earth. Maybe this one shift in consciousness is what is needed in our modern world to change things for the better.

> We as parents need a collective agreement to no longer see our children as unknowing beings to be impressed and programmed with society's culture and limitations. Rather, to find our child's gift and nurture the dream that requires the highest kind of love – one that is volitional – based on the child's needs and potentials.
>
> *Nurture Your Child's Gift: Inspired Parenting*, Caron B. Goode (2001).

When I work with a family who has a boy who is inattentive, prone to impulsive behaviour and very disruptive at school, I check out three things from the building blocks. The first is the nutrition building block, to check what nasties he may be eating that could trigger his behaviour. Secondly, I check how much sleep he is getting; the healthy boundaries building block is always next. The third is meaningful involvement; often by getting Dad to take him to the park twice a week to kick a football or a soccer ball, his behaviour turns around completely. This is an holistic solution-finding approach to benefit not just the child but also the family who has to live with that child. This common sense approach takes a more time than medication, however a long-term change needs to work for everyone. Traditional communities did not have medications in the form of pills, so common sense would suggest there must be a solution that is more closely aligned to the greater good of the community.

Please be a positive, meaningful part of a child's life other than your own. One of the greatest compliments I have had was to be the person a dear friend chose to leave her two year old with when on her way to the hospital to give birth to her next child. Her husband just handed me a sleepy child who was all crumpled up in her warm blanket and then drove away completely comfortable that their little girl would be well cared for. When this little one opened one eye to check what was happening, I caught a little smile on her lips and she slipped back to sleep. It was a moment etched deep in my mind and which still makes me feel blessed on all levels.

Parent Tips for Creating Meaningful Involvement

- *Being surrounded by caring, responsive adults is essential for young children.*

- *Primary caregivers have a bond of affection for children, for them to feel safe and loved.*

- *Meaningful involvement involves trust and unconditional, positive regard.*

- *Children need to feel they belong.*

- *Being fully present is vital for children of all ages.*

- *Solidarity and collective parenting is healthy for families and children.*

- *Positive, caring adults can help children learn life skills.*

- *The more adults in your family circle who can be meaningfully involved, the better for everyone.*

- *Volunteer for a school or community mentor program.*

- *Be careful to avoid learned helplessness, suppression and indulgence.*

- *See every child as a gift or a miracle.*

Children in traditional communities have the freedom to co-exist beside other members of their community. They play in the natural world, and they eat and sleep close by the main centre of the community. There are very clear boundaries about age appropriate behaviour, and while they are children, consistent routines and rituals support their growth and development. This predictability changes once they reach adolescence when the boys and girls spend more time learning how to become men and women. Clear boundaries are respected and valued to keep children safe and protected.

Building Block 7
Clear boundaries

There is no such thing as a perfect parent or perfect child. Decisions are made according to the circumstance and the current knowledge at the time.

Social shifts create less time with our children; less time to nurture their emotional growth and to instil the firm boundaries needed for the healthy growth of a moral and social code that helps in later life. Healthy, consistent boundaries help reduce uncertainty and chaos in children's lives and build predictability. They need to start from birth and be consistent for each child in a family. When the human brain follows certain rituals or behaviours it is unstressed and able to focus on the activity. Children like to anticipate their world and feel secure when they can predict coming events.

Key boundaries in childhood that influence our emotional competencies in relationships
• Physical safety from external danger, for example, fire or busy roads. • Freedom from adult abuse—verbal, emotional, physical and sexual. • Honouring respect and reverence. • Having physical needs met, for example, food, water and sleep. • Freedom from sibling and peer abuse and bullying. • Freedom from being ignored. • Protection from major change, or social dislocation. • Predictability in day to day living. • Parenting that allows children to experience mistakes or failure. • Letting children be children. • Acknowledging feelings and emotions.

There are some key areas where boundaries and routines play an important role in children's heath and well being and include:

- sleep
- meal times
- food choices
- school
- screen use—TV/computer/Internet
- the "I want" mentality
- childhood versus adolescence versus adulthood
- safety—physical, verbal and emotional
- bullying
- movies, TV shows and DVDs.

Sleep

In a recent article in *The Weekend Australian* titled, *The Lost Hour* researchers have determined that today's children from preschool to high school are sleeping an average of one hour less than 30 years ago; this is partly due to over-scheduling, burdensome homework, lax bedtimes, TV and mobile phones in the bedroom. Sleep scientists have now been able to determine the disastrous effect that lack of sleep has on developing brains. They now believe that sleep disorders can impair children's IQ just as much as lead exposure. Tired children cannot remember what they have just learned. Also, sleep loss impacts on the prefrontal cortex that is responsible for the executive function of the brain. Among its functions are thoughts to fulfil a goal, the prediction of outcomes and perceiving consequences of actions. Poor impulse control and poor problem solving are very common with tired children. Another key finding from the research showed that the more you learned during the day, the more you need to sleep during the night so that the brain can process and consolidate the memories. These are vital gene activities that also need to occur during REM to ensure synaptic plasticity, or the strengthening of neural connections.

Consistent boundaries around sleep are important for everyone. Sleep deprivation and inconsistent bed times impact on learning, mood moderation and behaviour. The brain needs deep sleep to renew cells and grow new neurons for learning. Good sleep also contributes to better emotional stability and a more agreeable demeanour.

Meal Times

Toddlers and children like to have clear boundaries around meal times and patterns. When established early in life in a positive way they can build family rituals that nourish children on many levels. Can you imagine how confusing it could be for a child to have dinner one night at 5.30 and the next night around 8.00, and the next night 6.30? Not only do regular times and patterns help children they help everyone in the family. Some rituals could be that dinner is eaten around the table, while breakfast can be at the kitchen bench. I encourage the evening meal to be a time of family gathering—whether or not you have a table. It encourages the communion or connectedness of a family group, and helps children learn how to be patient and understand simple dining etiquette. Remember that your children will save their worst dining behaviour for the home environment—they are learning how to behave with manners, however they save it for other tables.

> Real and lasting happiness comes through the progressive accumulation of lovely memories and special moment and the best way to be really successful in life is to be really kind.
>
> *The Monk Who Sold His Ferrari: A Fable About Fulfilling Your Dreams and Reaching Your Destiny*, Robin Sharma (1999).

Food Choices

Food choices also require firm boundaries. Adults create the food dynamics of children so it is important that they hold the high ground. It is easy to indulge children for peace, however the peace is short lived after a sugary treat (see Building Block 2 on nutrition).

For fussy eaters there should be clear choices about what they can eat if they refuse to eat the food that has been prepared—fruit is a healthy boundary. If over-processed, salty or sweet food choices are unavailable in the home, it makes it much harder for children to make poor choices while they are at home. They same goes for sweet drinks including fruit drinks—if they are unavailable, the children will not be able to fill up on these empty calories that mess with their bodies and brains.

School

At school, children need to behave according to a clear set of rules that ensure everyone's safety. Children who have not experienced firm boundaries will struggle in the structured school environment. Often, it is better to leave the school and the child to deal with issues around breaking school rules. This will teach them to take responsibility for their own actions, which is important in developing life resilience. Necessary emotional and social development may be delayed if parents intervene inappropriately when their child is being disciplined.

The homework issue is one that can cause enormous angst in some homes. While there is very little research that demonstrates that homework improves learning outcomes at school, it is considered as a necessary evil by most primary schools. Allow your children (over 10 years of age) to learn that homework is their responsibility without you needing to urge or nag them to do it. Also know that if you have a family event like a grandparent visiting for a couple of days, you are well within your parental rights to let your children's teacher know that no homework will be done during the visit. Family connectedness is precious and comes before maths worksheets and spelling lists. The same went for my sons' birthdays when they were in primary school; that was their special day, and unless they particularly wanted to do homework, they had a free night.

Use of Screens

Boundaries are important around the use of TVs and computers. When children watch TV it means they are not playing and interacting with others during this time—which is sometimes for up to five hours. Immersion in the virtual reality world can create distortions in a child's ability to determine what is real and what is not. The passivity of the activity may also set up patterns of physical lethargy later in life. Allowing children to have a television in their own bedroom creates a pattern of separation from the family. This may create an irreparable gap and make the teenage years more challenging.

> "In a sense, just as children's developing brains intrinsically expect that eyes will see light and ears will hear sound because of their developmental self-organisation, so also do children's developing minds and hearts expect that adults will talk in special ways to them and that caregivers will nurture them as they mature. Normal human development draws upon these natural and unrehearsed features of everyday early experience far more than it requires special educational toys, Mozart CDs, or flashcards."
>
> Judy Radich, Early Childhood Australia, speech 2006.

Do not be fooled by advertisers—children do not need TV programs or DVDs to learn or to be stimulated. As I have already mentioned there is plenty of research that suggests over-exposure to screens increases your child's chances of developing hyperactivity and inattentiveness. I have had to work with children who have been spooked by watching DVDs with their family that were simply too scary for them. Some were considered by many parents to be OK for kids like *Harry Potter* and *Lord of the Rings*. How can adults know how sensitive a young child's mental and emotional processing abilities are? This early damage can set your child up for anxiety issues and problems for life. Be vigilant and keep your developing child's mind protected from visual and auditory sensory attacks by the entertainment world.

The avoidance of violent films and computer games is also a very important boundary parents need to maintain. There are many research studies that validate that aggressive and violent games change the behaviour of children. Why would you want your child to be exposed to such damage psychologically? Aggression that becomes part of a child's behaviour is difficult to change once it appears and it will follow them through life. Many men and women in prison today are there because of a spontaneous violent incident—often a combination of an inability to manage their emotional world, and an aggressive nature or history.

Technology and the Internet can be problematic for children and parents. Children are unintentionally exposed to pornographic sites, while others have become victims of cyberspace bullying via emails and mobile phones. Experts recommend that a child does not have a computer before at least seven years of age (Eric Jensen). Real learning and development that children get from playing and physical activity in the first seven years is vital in building resilience. Always keep your computer in a common area so that adult supervision is close by. Keep time limits on the use of the computer because children can waste hours of valuable time that can be better spent playing outside or interacting with real people! Make sure you connect your child to a local library and make sure they know that finding information out by "googling" it on their PC is not the best or most accurate way to discover new knowledge!

The "I want" Mentality

Apply boundaries around "I want" demands when your children are young. Instant gratification and indulgence breeds a neediness attitude to life. This may also lead to an early introduction to the pressures of the consumer driven world of needing to look like everyone else.

There is more money spent by advertisers to capture the preschool consumer mind than is spent trying to cure childhood cancer. The most commonly recognised symbol in the world is the McDonalds golden M. One of the main dangers in this area is commercial television. Research studies show that children are deeply influenced by the advertising they are exposed to. One study gave a group of children shopping trolleys to fill with products they would like to buy. Every item they selected was something that was advertised on commercial television. Advertising is simply used to sell products and it often distorts the truth. Many of the cereals advertised are full of sugar, salt and so over-processed they have minimal nutritional value. They are made to look good for you; and also feature impossibly happy families eating cheerfully in tidy middle class kitchens. I totally support the complete banning of advertising for junk foods and nutritionally poor products of any kind. We must support parents to help children develop healthier food and exercise habits.

Please support the Kids First Campaign that is working to have serious additives banned in Australia. These dangerous additives have been banned in the UK from 2009 and they are found in foods like muesli bars, fruit juice and yogurt and have been linked to serious intellectual impairment in children and behavioural abnormalities. For more information visit www.additive alert.com.au

Occasional treats will never cause serious damage to children and they can help sweeten family celebrations and events. However still choose wisely and avoid colourings and highly salted or sweet foods in large quantities. Junk type foods are high in fat and can create a sense of well being that although temporary can create habits that stay with children for life.

One more thing around the "I want" mentality involves the building of the emotional competence by delaying gratification. This is a difficult one to learn, however it can be very helpful in life—especially if you plan to study, or save for a deposit on a house. There is something wonderful that can happen when a long awaited goal is realised or achieved. Many children today never master this competence because the instant nature of the world where 'now' is more important

Next birthday or Christmas please think carefully when buying your children gifts. Will they enhance your child's emotional, social and spiritual growth or will it have a detrimental effect?

Tips for Buying Gifts for Children

- *Will the gift create more conflict in the home with sibling rivalry?*
- *Does the gift meet a special interest in your child's life?*
- *Is the gift honourable to our earth—for example packaging—or does it build respect for our natural world?*
- *Does the gift allow for the growth of creativity?*
- *Is the gift locally made?*
- *Does the gift stimulate sharing or promote building emotional competencies like patience or learning to lose?*
- *Does the gift numb or stimulate the imagination?*
- *Will the gift encourage shared activity or solo activity?*
- *Always give at least one fantastic novel or picture book that stimulates reading.*
- *Does the gift encourage laughter and lightness?*
- *Does the gift honour childhood rather than promote getting older quicker? For example, padded bras for six year olds.*
- *Does the gift require or encourage being outside and away from the couch?*
- *Does the gift encourage physical activity for fun?*
- *Could the gift encourage the growth of personal responsibility? For example, a pet like a guinea pig, rat or goldfish?*
- *Have you donated to those less fortunate and let your children know why?*
- *Does the gift create shared play opportunities with mum, dad, grandma or grandad?*
- *Does the gift make really annoying noises that will drive you mad after one hour?*
- *If possible, make a gift from your own hands.*
- *Finally, always include little presents that cost a little. Most of the fun is in the anticipation and in the unwrapping.*

Boundaries Between Childhood and Adulthood

No one tells you about the potential damage of modern culture when you are expecting your first child. Steve Biddulph wrote the following words in Jane Bartlett's book, *Parenting with Spirit*:

> We want our children to grow up happy, healthy, strong and kind. But that isn't what the world wants. The world wants them greedy insecure, selfish, shallow and vain—to eat this junk food, and buy those clothes, watch this TV show, crave that magazine. Never knowing peace or feeling satisfaction. So, almost from the minute you first cradle your baby in your arms, you are at war.

Modern culture without boundaries can be very potentially damaging and its influence can be insidious and invisible until suddenly you wonder how your delightful and beautiful daughter turned into Princess Bitchface, as Dr Michael Carr-Gregg labels some challenging young teenage and pre teenage girls he has met in his work.

I encourage all parents and people who work with children to remember that children are children; they have immature emotional literacy, gaps in their understanding about their needs and wants, and all of them wish to be loved and valued exactly as they are, not how they could be. This is normal for children, and many of the concerns around children may stem from the pressures of living in our chaotic world and of perceiving children in a very different way to our ancient ancestors. We all need to step back from judging and criticising how children grow and develop—even children with special needs are still children who need play, fun and laughter to help them enjoy life. There are no quick fixes to raising children to be decent human beings. No magic pills or potions; it takes time, love and tenderness.

Children are quick to forgive, respond even quicker to nurturing love and kindness, and are just a moment away from being magical if we protect them from the shallow and superficial things in life.

It Doesn't Matter

It doesn't matter what a child
Looks like
Smells like
Thinks like
They still feel.

It doesn't matter what a child
Learns like
Speaks like
Behaves like
They still listen.

It doesn't matter who a child's parent's are
Where they live
How much money they have
What culture they follow
Children don't care.

What does matter in the lives
Of children,
Yours, mine and others
Is that we feel, we listen and we care.

Children are seedlings in the garden of life
They need sunshine and warmth
When they are cold and sad;
They need water and nourishment
When they are thirsty and hungry
They need attention and care
When they are challenged by life
And they need to be loved, appreciated
And held in awe of their potential
To be unique, beautiful and like no other.

Search for the hero within yourself
And then be there for our kids.
Please feel, listen and care
With your heart and soul and

You will become
A valued gardener in the
The garden of life and one day
A child may hold a special.
Memory of you forever
Hidden deep in their heart.

It Doesn't Matter, Maggie Dent, 2002.

If you are worried about a child, slow their life down, connect with them from where they are, play with them or simply be with them in our natural world. Take the stress away for just a short time and allow the child to be immersed in their imaginary world where children are meant to reside. They are only children for such a short time so let them be real kids in our unreal world.

Today's children are being hurried to grow up on many levels and one area that worries child experts increasingly is the sexualisation of our children. The consumer driven world that is being fed by the media and the Internet has distorted children's place in our world.

> The AS Board's approach to sexualised advertising material do not seem to take into account that it is never just one advertisement affecting children. Over the course of a childhood, it is cumulative exposure to hundreds or thousands of highly sexualised
> advertisements, with each advertisement often viewed multiple times, that affects children's development.
>
> Australian Institute's Paper, *Letting Children Be Children: Stopping the sexualisation of children in Australia*, Emma Rush and Andrea La Nauze, (2006).

Public opinion in Australia is certainly gaining momentum in opposing the destruction of childhood boundaries. Dr Karen Brooks in her latest book, *Popular Culture and Our Children* examines the role popular culture and, most importantly, parents play in creating children's ideas of themselves, and with unflinching frankness, questions the involvement of corporations that specifically target kids. This is refreshingly honest and revealing and well worth a read by any parent.

Another excellent book that explores the sexualisation of girls in Australia is, *What's Happening to Our Girls: Too Much, Too Soon* by Maggie Hamilton. Her book details the self-harm, the drinking, sexualisation of girls and their sexual experiences at early ages, the violence that they encounter and the eating disorders they suffer in depressing detail. By asking girls about what their friends were doing she discovered that shopping and sex were the two main powerful forces directing girls lives. How shallow and how sad?

Ms Hamilton discovered that girls found there was so much pressure to be a success and to be noticed, and very little about how to be resilient and how to cope with setbacks and adversity. Popularity has a great price when it turns poison—girls are very good at psychologically damaging other girls. They have taken bullying to a new level, especially with cyber bullying via email and SMS. This modern trend happens when we as a society does not invest in the holistic growth and development of children by ensuring boundaries are protected and values modelled. Emotional and social competence takes time to teach our children, and we are abandoning many children from having a healthy adult life by ignoring the damaging effects of modern culture. We must reclaim our children and take responsibility for their growth on all levels. We must not allow magazines, reality TV programs, sitcoms and the Internet as playing the role of 'super-parent' and shaping our children's characters and personalities.

In Maggie Hamilton's research for her book she discovered that all over the country school counsellors are now dealing with traumatised girls left to face the overwhelming fallout from the cruel and demeaning activities they participated in over the weekend. We must become more aware of this area of weakening of boundaries and protect both girls and boys pushing their boundary to adolescence until adolescence.

The words below come from Julie Gales' web site that she has set up to lift awareness of the dangers of modern culture, especially the media, on today's girls.

Each month twenty per cent of six-year-old girls and almost half of ten and eleven year old girls read at least one of the most popular girls' magazines—Barbie Magazine, Total Girl and Disney Girl. These magazines teach their young readers to dance in sexually provocative ways, to idolise highly sexualised young women such as Paris Hilton, Jessica Simpson and Lindsay Lohan, and to have crushes on adult male celebrities—all while they are still in primary school.

The capacity of children to develop healthy body image and self esteem is compromised by pressure to look like miniature adults. One particularly alarming manifestation of this is an apparent trend for young people to be hospitalised for severe eating disorders at younger ages, in an ironic twist on the childhood obesity issue. Children's general sexual and emotional development can be affected by exposure to advertising and marketing that is saturated with sexualised images and themes. To the degree that children focus on sexualising themselves rather than pursuing other more age-appropriate developmental activities, all aspects of their development may be affected. The sexualisation of children also risks normalising and possibly encouraging paedophilic sexual desire for children.

From the website Kids Free 2B Kids, http://www.kf2bk.com

During my global travels I am appalled at how parents have been seduced by the toy and clothing companies. The mentality that encourages young girls to wear padded bras, G-strings and skimpy clothes while wearing full make up to five year old birthday parties is insane. I had a friend share with me her horror at the preschool girls in her daughter's class all wearing full make up to a birthday party and teasing the girls without make up.

Preschool teachers tell me they hate hearing about what is happening on *Home and Away* when children tell news on the mat. Children are meant to wear adults clothes when dressing up—putting oranges into old bras to look grown up, and tottering in mum's or nanna's high heel shoes. This shows the girls that adulthood is a very long way away. One mother told me she thought her daughter looked cute with high heels and make up, however she went very quiet when I told her that girls who have their sexual boundaries distorted in childhood often end up sexually promiscuous by 12. I have worked with tweens under 14 years of age who have been involved sexually with men who thought they were much older. Once the sexual boundaries have been violated, they are very difficult if not impossible to rebuild.

> Children are meant to be children, looking like children, behaving like children, rather than little adults.

I believe we have neutered the role that caring fathers used to play in protecting their girls and pre-teens. Fathers used to (light heartedly) threaten to use the shot-gun if a young man taking his daughter out did not treat her right. Where there are fathers—or a strong, positive male presence—in the home, maybe we need to allow them to have a vital input as to what the girls of the house wear in public. The women of the house may have been seduced by the subtle pressures of modern magazines and the celebrity love affair, however dad knows boys and men—and they have not changed. He knows what looks 'slutty' or reads 'tart' and he has a very important role to protect his daughter. Yes, she may hate him until her pre frontal lobe grows in her 20s—but who said parenting was a popularity contest?

There are many anecdotal stories being told around schools about how modern girls are experimenting sexually very early by giving boys oral sex often on school buses and during school time. They appear to have the message about avoiding pregnancy, however they have missed the one about respecting yourself and valuing self-acceptance and appreciation. The desire to cheapen oneself in order to be popular has been influenced by the celebrity craze that borders on the ridiculous. Reality TV programs have a lot to answer for as well; the buck does not stop with the young pre-teens or teens, it stops with the adults they live with who have a pre frontal lobe of their brain that is supposed to make them smarter. While my husband was doing his usual channel surfing one evening we saw a small part of the final show of the last Australian *Big Brother* program two 10–12 year old girls were interviewed in the audience, and they admitted how much they loved the show and that they had not missed one episode.

I once confiscated a Dolly magazine from a year 8 girl in one of my English classes in 1998. Their target market is 12–15 years of age. The leading article was, *How to have multiple orgasms*. Why do 12–14 year old girls need to know about that? This is an excellent example of inappropriate material for pre and pubescent girls. On the other hand, I was 43 and I found some of the article quite interesting and helpful.

Kaz Cooke has written a very comprehensive book titled, *Girls Stuff* which has been promoted across Australia as the new must have bible for girls. I have had a number of mothers speak to me about how shocked and horrified they were with the inappropriate nature of some of the material for girls under 15. One mother told me how her 12 year old daughter saved up to buy the book because her school promoted it; when she took it to read in private, she became very quiet. It took a few days before she brought the book out to her Mum and said it made her feel really uncomfortable. Her mother read it and she too found parts of it very confronting. I congratulate Kaz on her courage to write a modern book that explores key issues for girls today, however parents need to still be the vigilant primary carer who determines when their daughter will be ready to absorb or need that type of in-depth information.

An ABC radio presenter interviewed a producer of a planned new TV series called *Dirt Girls*. This series is for the girls who just never got into Bratz or Barbie dolls, and who preferred to be outside in the dirt, building cubbies and exploring the real world. I felt a sense of relief that a quality program is coming that will explore a more naturally grounded way for a girl to be a girl in our modern world. The shallow, indulgent and self-centred pattern of behaviour of those girls who have been reared on the belief that their looks and whether they put out for the boys, are more important than their character and their potential in life, have a tough ride in front of them. Their parents sadly have been conned by the insanity of the modern Western world.

Strategies for Parents and Caregivers

- Tell your children from a very early age often, that they are loved for who they are, not for how they look.
- As they get older, help them understand that beliefs that link beauty with happiness and success are mistaken.
- With adolescents, explain that ads designed to make you think that being sexy is the same as being successful are not true.
- Minimise children's exposure to commercial media and kids' magazines.
- Don't buy skimpy clothing or bras for young children.
- Write to department stores to complain, and applaud, where good clothing choices are offered.

http://www.kf2bk.com

Bullying Revisited

Bullying is a very hot topic in Australia, and I know it is a very real issue around the Western world from my travels, especially to the UK and USA. I can write with some authority about bullying as I was a victim in my home environment and a completely awful bitch and a bully at school.

Bullies are often created in the early years of life. Frontal lobe development ensures emotional maturity; it is an essential brain development and needs very particular care and nurturing in the first two years. During this time there is growth in the nerve pathways that underpin learning and language development, and establish anti-anxiety chemical systems in the brain. This young brain is very susceptible to stress and distress. Warm attentive parenting will help a baby or toddler repeatedly activate the release of the positive soothing chemicals oxytocin and opioids that counteract the cortisol of the distress response. The young brain is largely run by the primitive responses from the lower or reptilian brain and those feelings overwhelm easily our small children.

> When a child is not given enough help with his intense lower brain feelings and primitive impulses, his brain may not develop the pathways to enable him to manage stressful situations effectively. The legacy later in life is that he will not develop the higher human capacity for concern, or the ability to reflect on his feelings in a self aware way. Brain scans show that many violent adults are still driven, just like infants, by their ancient rage/fear and defence/attack responses deep in their brain.
>
> Margot Sunderland.

Here are some ways to best support essential brain development that will help children grow into caring people without a need to bully others:

- *Create a caring bond as soon as possible with lots of skin to skin contact; soothing when obviously distressed—not when the bottom lip quivers; enormous amounts of comfort touch such as rocking to sleep when they are distressed; singing soothing lullabies; tender stroking; pushing the pram backwards and forwards; simple, genuine loving attention.*
- *Create pathways of comfort with sheepskins, cuddly blankets, soft toys, their hands or thumbs and maybe a comforter dummy.*
- *Involve others to help in the first two years only if they can be loving, caring and comfortable with safe, nurturing touch.*
- *Avoid forcing young ones when they are experiencing separation distress—this hurts a young child much like a physical pain. There are some key studies that link separation in early life to depression.*

- *Large based day-care centres are unable to meet the emotional and nurturing needs of babies and very young children; there is much evidence that shows extensive, long day-care early on is contributing to more aggression and non-compliance in children.*
- *Healthy management of parent emotions and the use of the right voice and energy—being calm, enthusiastic and optimistic is really helpful.*
- *Ensure opportunity for respite for parents; everyone benefits with a little break from parenting young children; ensure children are only with people they love, or who are able to offer a gentle loving care.*
- *Avoid shouting and criticism as it strengthens the lower brain patterns of distress, fear and rage.*
- *Routines bring children comfort and lower the risk of an emotional overload of fear or rage.*
- *Lower other potential stressors from babies and toddlers such as shopping centres, large social gatherings, too much activity or over stimulation from TVs, DVDs, and very large toys with bells and whistles.*
- *Create healthy sleep cycles and patterns as soon as possible.*
- *Protect children from early bullies, whether they are older siblings or at day-care. Then teach them how to become assertive, not aggressive.*

Bullies may have immature brain development with an inability to communicate effectively which creates a habitual pattern of behaviour. Building significant, caring adults into a bully's life is vital in helping to heal these patterns. The brain has plasticity and can change over time, however it needs lots of tender loving care (TLC) to make this happen. Punishment and punitive critical behaviour management will fail as it is not supporting the growth of neurons in the upper brain.

If we remember all children simply want to be loved and accepted unconditionally then this is what bullies are secretly wanting too. The young brain before starting school has a much better potential for change to overcome early delays.

Unfortunately, our systems—especially education—have created such a serious phobia about safe touch that those vital warm, loving child care workers and teachers are unable to soothe and nurture children who desperately need it to help them manage their stressful and overwhelming negative feelings. In the UK they have 'Nurture Groups' in some schools with people who are trained in safe touch and reassuring nurturing; they work closely with children with serious behavioural patterns so that they are able to gain essential emotional and social skills in order to re-join regular classrooms.

Bullies and victims both need support but rarely receive what they need with our current systems. Emotional growth needs trust, respect and appropriate support, and only specially trained people with a kind, caring disposition will achieve that. If our modern world continues to put work and wealth ahead of the vital early years of children's lives, we will continue to despair at the increasing violence and aggression in our communities. Schools will simply continue to be left to manage the results of unhealthy parenting, and the disruption that occurs both inside and outside the classroom.

Sadly, children from loving, caring homes get penalised because their learning environment is disrupted by emotionally and socially incompetent children. Teachers are struggling with unreachable and unteachable children—who later become adults with the same low emotional and social competencies and struggle to find a place  to belong. Healing our world begins from the cradle to preschool.

A personal growth expert once told me that he felt bullies and victims both have serious issues with how they perceive boundaries. He believed that children learn this from their primary caregivers within the family. Until they are able to respect their personal boundaries without using too much or too little power, they will continue in their pattern.

I once had a well known school bully in a class I inherited from another teacher. I refused to buy into the expectation that he and other staff had of him, and I spent the usual time at the beginning of term building safety in the classroom. One of the ways, I did that was having paired sharing opportunities; a technique I learned from Jack Canfield when I trained with him in 1998. When the term started no one would sit next to the bully out of fear. By week three I noticed that he sometimes had people sitting next to him, and soon he was just a part of the class. He never had a bullying incident during that whole term. During a circle time at the end of term a classmate asked how come he hadn't been thrown out of class or been busted all term. He replied quite quickly, "This is the first time in a class I haven't been treated like a piece of shit." Human connectedness in a safe environment has a huge potential to heal the worst bully.

The self esteem or self concept of a bully or a victim must change in order for their behaviour to change. This takes repeated experiences that challenge their core concepts and beliefs, which takes time and patience. The brain's plasticity will allow new neural wiring to occur over time. If this opportunity does not present itself, the chances of initiating life long change is not high, however there is always hope.

To conclude this chapter on boundaries, I am including a story that I think sums up why parents who maintain beautiful boundaries are important.

Mean Mums

We had the meanest mum in the whole world! While other kids ate lollies for breakfast, we had to have cereal, eggs, and toast. When others had softdrink and a lamington for lunch, we had to eat sandwiches. And you can guess our mother fixed us a dinner that was different from what other kids had, too.

Mum insisted on knowing where we were at all times. You'd think we were convicts in a prison. She had to know who our friends were, and what we were doing with them. She insisted that if we said we would be gone for an hour, we would be gone for an hour or less.

We were ashamed to admit it, but she had the nerve to break the Child Labour Laws by making us work. We had to wash the dishes, make the beds, learn to cook, vacuum the floor, do laundry, and all sorts of cruel jobs. I think she would lie awake at night thinking of more things for us to do.

She always insisted on us telling the truth the whole truth, and nothing but the truth. By the time we were teenagers, she could read our minds.

Then, life was really tough! Mum wouldn't let our friends just honk the horn when they drove up. They had to come up to the door so she could meet them. While everyone else could date when they were 12 or 13, we had to wait until we were 16.

Because of our mum we missed out on lots of things other kids experienced. None of us have ever been caught shoplifting, vandalising other's property, or ever arrested for any crime. It was all her fault.

Now that we have left home, we are all God-fearing, educated, honest adults. We are doing our best to be mean parents just like mum was.

I think that's what's wrong with the world today. It just doesn't have enough mean mums anymore.

Source: Internet

Tips for Parents on Boundaries

- *Boundaries give children predictability and a sense of order in their lives, and reduce the stress that comes from uncertainty.*

- *Boundaries build character and a personal and moral template to navigate the world.*

- *Parents need to have the courage to be strong and vigilant in maintaining boundaries.*

- *Children are meant to be children—especially under 10. Avoid hurrying up your children's childhood.*

- *Children spell love T-I-M-E.*

- *Create a supportive network of aware parents who will help keep children safe from certain aspects of the modern world.*

- *Avoid media that sexualises children or promotes products that have potential for harm.*

- *Let the child within you enjoy your children.*

Stress was seldom a regular feature in traditional tribal communities. The whole community were committed to the safety and well being of everyone else no one was marginalised because of their age, gender, special needs or lack of ability. The main source of stress is driven by sensing a lack of control, and traditional tribal people never attempted to control nature, the source of all sustenance.

They simply accepted how everything was and worked together to make the best of each day as it came. The men were responsible for the protection and provision of large prey. They would respond to threat as nature intended by becoming chemically aroused to run fast, or fight bravely. Once the primary threat had passed, their high stress levels would simply disappear.

Building Block 8
Absence of stress

The absence of stress is an important preventive factor in building resilience. It is essential in the early years for helping our children grow and develop as healthy as possible on all levels.

> Increasingly, scientists are linking stress in infancy and childhood to the soaring numbers of people suffering from anxiety and depressive and disorders from adolescence onward.
>
> Margot Sunderland.

I receive many emails from concerned parents about children who are struggling emotionally and socially. Modern life is really putting pressure, usually invisible, on our children—especially sensitive children. Children's brains are immature and unable to cope with the stressors of modern adult living and often misinterpret adult challenges as being about them or their fault. Consistent stress becomes distress and the brain is seriously affected. Irrational behaviour, unstable emotions, sleeplessness and defiance are potential signs that a child is stressed, and struggling. The brain will focus on its survival needs and within a week brain cells halve in their production and many begin to wither. This means that learning and concentration will be impeded, and this can be very frustrating for children, especially in the school environment. Until a child feels safe this can continue. Calm, quiet home environments can help ease the symptoms of stress.

Tips to Calm Your Home

- *Remove clutter and mess because it can add to a child's perception of being in chaos and out of control.*
- *Play music that soothes the brain—anything from Classical to nature sounds.*
- *Ensure boundaries are clear and healthy around meals, sleep, siblings and safety.*
- *Take children out into the fresh air as often as possible.*
- *Use calming aromatherapies.*
- *Practice small acts of kindness and generosity.*
- *Use quiet voices and ask politely rather than demand.*
- *Really listen to your children—without interrupting.*
- *Use safe touch through foot or back massages.*
- *Use life enhancing language that encourages a positive mind set.*
- *On a nightly basis use calming, creative visualisations for everyone.*
- *Stimulate more play and creativity.*
- *Have a teddy bear's picnic purely for fun.*

Chronic stress is also known as distress. Mild stress can be beneficial in terms of brain development and growth. However, prolonged periods of stress can impact deeply on the growth of brain cells, the size of the brain cells and the individual's ability to learn.

> When we feel too stressed we are less likely to show exploratory, curious, novelty seeking behaviours.

Research shows that social dislocation can be highly stressful for individuals. Moving preschools, schools, homes or countries may be contributing to a retardation or delay in some children's intellectual, social and emotional growth. Distress can cause long term damage to the brain's adaptive systems and these are crucial for resilient behaviour like decision making, reflection and flexible thinking. Studies clearly link distress with lowered cognitive capacity.

The early years are critical because of rapid brain growth. The impact of early distress, especially from abandonment, threats or violence, may lead to brain impairment. A child will be more likely to suffer from depression, stress and anxiety disorders, and have a lower IQ.

Setting boundaries and being consistent carers with similar expectations of how to behave, helps reduce stress for toddlers and children. It is very confusing for children when they receive different instructions and discipline. Stress is a response to the perception of lack of control. Children are susceptible to stress because they seldom have much control over their environment.

> An essential component of resilience and high self esteem is the belief that one has some control over what is occurring in one's life.

Help toddlers and young children understand that they have a sense of autonomy and some influence about how they function. Early decision making and problem solving is very helpful because it builds a sense of empowerment that is beneficial in later life. Making simple choices about whether to wear the red or the blue t-shirt helps build this emerging autonomy. Without choices children can feel resentful, angry, powerless and prone to rebellious behaviour.

It is important to avoid too many rules because they can create a 'police state'. Ensure that the rules set are easy to remember and follow, and that everyone in the family knows them. Identify five key guidelines that work well, and as they grow older you may need to add new ones to the list. Always use calm voices and do not threaten when you are trying to create a stress free environment. Allow plenty of spaces for child-directed activities because it helps children to feel in control of their world.

Quietness, silence and stillness are important in children's lives. These are times when there is no noise, no specific activity and a space from the business of their daily lives. These quiet times allow the brain to come offline to sort and process new learning and to explore how things fit together in their minds. Memory and thinking are both enhanced with quietness.

Moments of calmness allow children to experience the state of absorbed play, where they become so absorbed by what they are doing that they lose track of time. This is an experience of 'oneness' within themselves and a total absence of stress. This quiet place within is valuable later in life when experiencing adversity. It helps us understand how to navigate our way out of challenges, and access our inner wisdom, not just the cognitive, rational mind.

All parents want the best for their children, however we now know that some children will not be successful at school in an academic sense. This will include children who have learning difficulties, hyperactivity problems, special needs—whether they be physical, mental or emotional—and those who have come to school without the vital development required in the early years. These children are still going to grow up and become adults in our societies around the world, and education and schooling should involve the whole child. All children need caring guidance to grow and mature. They need to have safe learning environments where they can learn how to socialise, play and learn basic literacy and numeracy skills.

All students need to learn how to learn. They need to learn how to think, interpret the world and people, and to make sense of experiences. The very best learning environments will help children identify their unique skills or strengths, while helping them also identify their weaknesses. The very best classrooms happen when students feel safe enough to work cooperatively with others to iron out individual differences, with strengths.

Many schools are war zones for students of all ages. Sometimes it's because of too many students in too small an area—which can be very threatening for smaller students. Older students with inadequate self-concepts may need to bully other students— always the ones they perceive as weaker. Then there are those scary places called school toilets. My sons would never go into school toilets and there was a frantic rush for the toilets when we arrived home every afternoon. These places are often dark wet and a place to hide from figures of authority, so the troubled students often gather there. Awful things happen in school toilets, and so an enormous stress for many students is, "Will I be able to wait until I get home?"

Another hidden stressor for students is finding a safe place to play. Children need safe spaces to play with their friends as the power struggles in playgrounds come and go— these struggles are always lurking in the back of children's minds. Many marginalised students wander around avoiding groups of students to avoid conflict, or they hide in the library.

In classrooms it is sometimes hard for teachers to have a healthy amount of challenge in learning tasks without putting students off through that deep, irrational fear of failure. It can be very scary in a classroom with a teacher who has lost control—it is especially scary for the well behaved students. They can get caught between having to choose supporting their fellow students or protecting the teacher. Noisy classrooms threaten auditory learners, and over-controlled classrooms antagonise kinaesthetic learners. Then there are horrid working environments that are too hot and stuffy, or freezing cold. Some classrooms have vomit coloured carpets and peeling paint and these environments make positive learning outcomes very difficult to achieve.

I have tried to show some of the causes of stress and anxiety that occur in students' lives so that parents may have more empathy when they get a grunt to that old question, "How was school today?" Home can be a refuge from the pressures of school and all students need transition time from school to home. The brain needs to relax a little from being on guard all day; they need time to eat something and allow the body to shift gears into a more comfortable emotional state. So treat your children with kindness, and save your questions for later when they have swapped 'codes' and they have given their bodies and minds time to process their busy day. Rushed or non-existent transition times can cause children and teenagers to become emotionally overwhelmed, increasing the chance of angry or aggressive behaviour. Do you have fights in the car on the way home from school? Has your child had problems on the bus bringing them home, or have you had some concerns in their after school care? Try to give them some 'chill-out' time and a healthy chance to transition from school.

I was delighted to see a front page story in, *The Sydney Morning Herald* about the research from Dr Margaret Sims on how they can measure the stress levels of children in child care. Part of her research showed that children from loving homes are stressed when placed in poor, quality child care centres, yet children from disadvantaged families are better off in child care, even if the quality is substandard. Dr Sims measured the cortisol levels by using saliva tests on the children. She went on to say that chronically high cortisol levels were implicated in long term health and behavioural problems. For more information on Margaret's study visit the website at www.psychology.ecu.edu.au/staff/cv/sims_m.php.

This study would fit in with my commonsense approach to parenting and education—the better the care, the healthier the child. A high quality centre is characterised by warm, responsive and respectful staff/child relationships and good communication between parents and staff. Funny, because exactly the same happens in school and high school! Daniel Goleman also believes that happy, calm children learn best.

Parent Tips for Managing Stress

- *Chronic stress causes changes in the brain.*

- *Children benefit from calm quiet spaces in their world.*

- *Being rushed and hurried causes stress for children.*

- *Allow children time just 'to be' and not always busy.*

- *Children sense their parents' stress and react to it.*

- *Calmness can be learned.*

- *Avoid too much noise and visual stimulation in homes.*

- *Avoid too much exposure to TVs, computers and other electronic games.*

- *Create safe home environments with boundaries and routines.*

- *Avoid too much significant change in children's lives.*

- *Feeling pressured causes cortisol levels to rise in children.*

- *Soothing and reassuring children triggers oxytocins and calms children.*

Within traditional communities survival of the community was the primary concern. Children played a vital part in that survival. They were able to participate meaningfully in gathering wood, water and food. This responsibility was a normal part of childhood. They were encouraged to become self sufficient and independent. They were able to feel they were a worthwhile and valued part of their community because of this. Children were also able to develop mastery in other recreational areas that took their interest, while they were still children.

Building Block 9
Self mastery

> Children cannot push themselves on until they have done very thoroughly what it is they need to do. Until they have reached the state of boredom they are still motivated by unfinished business and can't move on. Boredom when they finally attain it provides the push to move on – but the push comes from within – not without.
>
> Janet Gonzalez-Mena et al.

Self mastery naturally progresses in the absence of stress. Achievement and success build an authentic sense of self esteem and self value. Even being able to do up buttons is self mastery. Life is a continual journey of self discovery, growth and the realisation of more of our human potential. Children need to have others to help them become competent and taste success so they can take it into adulthood.

From around two years of age, toddlers are capable of learning simple practical skills as well as social skills that will strengthen their life coping skills. They are starting to develop their sense of 'self' and need for autonomy and personal independence. The stronger a person's sense of identity and independence, and the life skills that support these attributes, the better their resilience.

It is important for parents and carers to provide many varied physical and mental activities for their children to experience before they start school. School presents the opportunity to learn new skills, and children who have had positive, interactive early childhoods tend to learn better.

> Always help a child make the most of the abilities he or she already has, and don't focus on the disability.
>
> Janet Gonzalez-Mena et al.

No one person is excellent at everything. With the understanding of multiple intelligences we now recognise that we have innate abilities and talents, and ones that we need to work on. I am incredibly spatially challenged—always getting lost in shopping centres, large toilets, hotels and unfamiliar places. I have difficulty with telling my left from my right, and frequently lose my car in car parks. (Thank goodness you can make the tail lights flash in modern cars, it has helped me so much locate my lost car!) Given that adults have these individual differences, the same goes for children when they are learning skills and tasks.

Basic literacy is very important in developing resilience because the ability to read and write increases the chances of life success. We need a basic level of literacy to read road maps, emails, SMS, fill in application forms and other documents or contracts. Literacy begins very early with reading to, and having conversations with, young children. This takes take time and effort and cannot happen in a week. Children not only pick up nuances of language patterns, they learn to sit still and listen. To master these skills before preschool is really helpful for children and happens largely from plenty of interaction with adults and other children.

It is helpful if you can develop an interest in storytelling in the early years. Having special story books that become favourites helps children develop a passion for special stories. One of my sons loved *Franklin the Turtle*. He had nearly all the books and his special favourites were, *Franklin Gets Lost* and *Franklin Afraid of the Dark*. When it came to packing up the family home and moving my 14 year old son was not quite ready to have his

Franklin books packed away into storage. They were kept in a drawer in his new abode. He highly valued his special books from his childhood; they were keepers of memories.

> For as long as he could remember
> Wombat had wanted to be in the Nativity.
> Now, at last, he was old enough to take part.
> So, with his heart full of hope
> And his head full of dreams,
> He hurried along to the auditions.
>
> *Wombat Divine*, Mem Fox (1995).

Mastery can happen in small ways for children—sometimes almost unnoticed—and parents can never quite tell when they have mastered something. One day they may be able to drink easily out of a cup, and the next day spill it everywhere. Remaining encouraging and supportive is helpful, especially when they struggle to master a new skill like sharing toys or falling asleep easily.

Dr Louise Porter in her book, *Children are People Too: A parent's guide to young children's behaviour* expressed similar views around children's needs. She noticed the following four triggers in young children:

1. *Children are naturally exuberant and excitable and can crash into each other and hurt each other—often they feel a need to retaliate.*
2. *Children learn through exploration both physically and socially and some of their actions like throwing food on the floor are a result of this rather than a deliberate act of defiance.*
3. *Children under three years of age may not know any better—yet. They are still learning.*
4. *Sometimes children lose control of themselves—just like some adults do. Yes, they know what they should do, but they lose control—like a person on a diet who cannot resist a bucket of hot chips.*

Mastery takes practise and practise takes time. To master catching or kicking a ball a child needs to have lots of practise. They see this as play. Yes, you could be getting washing off the line or starting dinner instead of helping them master a new skill, however, time for helping them improve slips away quickly. Their self esteem is very dependent on acquiring competence and mastery and they need help from others often to do that. Sometimes kicking a football, shooting netball goals or searching for rare frogs in the dark are what parents need to do to help their child become competent at something. Conquering a new boundary like swimming faster, playing a recognisable tune on a piano, being able to cook a cake, or ride a bike without training wheels is essential in building a healthy sense of self. It teaches a key element of resilience—"I am capable."

> "When we do the best we can, we never know what miracle is wrought in our life, or in the life of another."
>
> Helen Keller

Many people have etched into their minds the day they rode their bicycles without training wheels. One grandmother came up to me once and said how true it was when a child mastered riding a bike without training wheels. The night before her 14 year old grandson with cerebral palsy had phoned very excited to tell Nan that he could finally ride his bike without training wheels. She said she cried with joy for his new mastery. The taste of sweet success becomes a healthy motivator for children to learn; they have also learned that mistakes can be corrected and overcome with persistence. These are very important emotional competences that children develop when they are young. Overcoming setbacks is a critical part of resilience.

> It is natural for parents to wish to insulate their children, to reduce the adversity, risk or stresses they may face. On the other hand too much protection, support or insulation may deprive children of opportunities to learn to deal with mistakes in affirmative, self-esteem enhancing ways.
>
> Robert Brooks and Sam Goldstein.

Hands-on experience is the best teacher for children, and sometimes this hands-on experience can lead to accidents or injuries. Few children have learned to ride their bicycles without a few skinned shins or knees.This is valuable real learning for children who learn to understand that we can recover and overcome setbacks. Real experience means that rather than telling children about vegetables and that they are grown in the ground, we create a patch or a tub and plant something with them. Children who have been taken to lots of interesting places learn so much faster and more comprehensively than those who have not. Allowing children opportunities to milk a cow, collect manure and pick strawberries creates lasting learning and shapes the way they see the world.

Young children develop in different ways and times, and parents and teachers need to be careful not to force developmental boundaries by urging children to master tasks prematurely. This is happening in some pre-schools where early childhood teachers are being asked to get children to take early reader books home. There are significant developmental parameters that must be respected or you may unintentionally teach your child they are a

failure, or dumb because they are not ready to tackle that task. Competence develops confidence and, unfortunately, the reverse is true as well. Despite the curriculum driven focus of early years education, children respond to the world in their own unique way, in their own time, and when they are in a safe and caring environment.

> Learning and success encompass so much more than getting ten out of ten for a spelling test. Learning and success are about inner happiness, intrinsic motivation and having the confidence and competence for discovery and learning.
>
> Kathy Walker.

Small acts of self mastery are just as important for children as the big ones, like riding a bike without training wheels, making a sandwich and doing a handstand. Some good ways to build confidence and concentration skills are through the small things that include mastering skipping, clapping games and singing. Jenny Mosley from the UK has some excellent resources that build these talents while having lots of fun. Check out her *Clapping Games* and *More Clapping Games* (with CDs), and know that children are wired to learn these simple activities much easier than adults. I struggle enormously because of my spatial issues, however even children with poor school performance can develop these skills quickly. This impacts on the self concepts because you cannot continue to believe that you are useless if you are brilliant at a skipping game or a clapping game. The other enormous plus from these games and activities is that they involve real human interaction.

Another excellent resource is *Songs with Movement* created by Leonie Cecich. Leonie's oldest son was born with Down's syndrome and she began to write songs to support his physical therapy. All of her songs have been written to help reinforce concepts set in place by occupational therapists, speech therapists, psychologists and physiotherapists in a fun and funky way. What Leonie found was that the songs and activities help all kids, especially those with special needs. These lyrics come from Leonie's, *The Goodbye Song* from her first, *You Gotta Get Up*.

The time has come to say farewell,
Give a hug and a smile and a wave as well.
Goodbye, goodbye!
Give a hug and a smile and a wave as well.

The time has come to say farewell,
Give a hug and a smile and a wave as well.
Goodbye, goodbye!
Give a hug and a smile and a wave as well.

We must not lose sight of the fact that humans have been raising children for over five million years. Much of the instinctual parental patterns are still valid today—they simply have a more complex context. When making decisions within your home ensure you ponder on what it may look like from your child's perspective. There is no perfect preparation for life and there is no perfect child. Maybe we could just simplify the process of parenting and caring for children in the early years. Judy Radich sums it up beautifully as, our challenge is to let go of some of our long-help beliefs and really engage with children and the world they live in (Early Childhood Australia Magazine, *Every Child*, p7, Vol 14, No 2, 2008).

"Most of us grew up speaking a language that encourages us to label, compare, demand and pronounce judgements rather than be aware of what we are feeling and needing. I believe life alienating communication is rooted in views of human nature that have exerted their influence for several centuries. These views stress our innate evil and deficiency and a need for education to control our inherently undesirable nature."

Marshall Rosenberg. 2000, p23

Helpful, positive communication skills used by parents really help children develop self mastery and conquer self doubt. It follows on from the need to be present with children: Both of these things are not rocket science and yet both are really important especially in the first 5 years of a child's life.

Being Heard

- *"Let me put this down so I can give you my full attention."*
- *"Wait a second while I turn off the TV/radio/computer so I can really hear you."*
- *"So what you mean is ..."*
- *"Did you do this all by yourself?"*
- *"Tell me more about this."*
- *"In other words..."*
- *"Let me see if I understand you so far..."*
- *"That must have been hard/easy/challenging for you!"*
- *"Are you open to some feedback from me?"*
- *"If you were to do that again, how could you improve what you achieved?"*
- *"Tell me when you would like me to help you."*
- *"Sometimes things just don't work out, and other times they do. This happens for us grown-ups too."*
- *"Mistakes can teach us important things. What can you learn from this?"*
- *"Try another way to solve this."*
- *"Breathe deeply until you can calm a little."*

Never forget that we keep learning and growing right through life. Self mastery is not just for kids; a vital part of adult's growth is learning to have humility when things they thought they had mastered go awry. This is something that allows children to feel safe; the capacity to allow vulnerability to appear as a normal part of meaningful relationships. My challenge to eat spaghetti bolognaise without having some drop on my generous bosom is something I am yet to master—this lack of ability has been the source of great mirth and delight within our family, and will continue to be so forever. Our children do not need for us to be perfect, just real and able to own life's little moments when they appear as they are, not as they could be.

10 Great Truths about Life that Little Children have Learned

1. No matter how hard you try, you cannot baptise cats.

2. When your Mom is mad at your Dad, don't let her brush your hair.

3. If your sister hits you, don't hit her back. They always catch the second person.

4. Never ask your three year old brother to hold a tomato.

5. You can't trust dogs to watch your food.

6. Don't sneeze when someone is cutting your hair.

7. Never hold a Dust-Buster and a cat at the same time.

8. You can't hide a piece of broccoli in a glass of milk.

9. Don't wear polka-dot underwear under white shorts.

10. The best place to be when you're sad is Grandpa's lap.

Source: Internet.

Parent Tips for Building Self Mastery

- *Hold the premise that every child ever born is a unique and special.*
- *Every child ever born has their own unique gifts and talents—every child is different.*
- *Multiple intelligences mean we have different ways of being smart.*
- *Find special interests when children are young and encourage these interests.*
- *Developing an internal locus of control is healthy. External ones like being competitive, the thinnest or that problems are always someone else's fault will result in personal challenge.*
- *Being able to express oneself and be heard are important in growing in self mastery.*
- *Allowing children to experience failure, and conflict helps them to develop strategies to overcome the same later in life.*
- *Life enhancing language will help children keep attempting a task until they master it.*
- *Small things are the big things—buttons, shoe laces, blowing noses successfully, mastering knife and fork, cleaning teeth, blowing bubbles, riding bikes, and climbing trees.*
- *Helping children grow in mastery takes lots of patience, time and many, many repeated attempts because children's brains are unable to comprehend what the adult brain can, and the plasticity of the brain takes time to wire new learning.*
- *Seeking and encouraging unique strengths in each sibling is important.*

- *Doing works better than telling, lecturing or nagging.*
- *Being enthusiastic without being overly pushy with children's accomplishments is tricky.*
- *Having high, positive expectations for our children is important without having unrealistic ones, especially one's we may never have fulfilled when we were children.*
- *As children get older, mastery in real tasks like cleaning shoes, making lunches, fixing things with dad, cooking, washing the car, attending to small cuts and grazes, addressing letters, painting, and even changing light bulbs helps children feel confident and competent. There is a window from 5–9 years of age where they love to help and by adolescence the novelty seems to leave.*
- *Encourage an awareness and respect of the environment and the natural world.*
- *Teach children how to make healthy snacks.*
- *Teach children some basic first aid.*
- *Teach children road rules when walking or riding a bike.*
- *Learn to comfort without paralysing—encourage more than you praise.*

Valuing the human spirit has been part of every traditional community. Profound and unconditional acceptance of each other regardless of age, gender, ability or status bonds people together. There is a strong sense of communion that is celebrated in small ways by sharing, caring and being. There are also shared gatherings of celebration that honour rites of initiation and the birth of new miracles- children. The natural world was seen as the source of all life and respected deeply. Many moments of deep awe and wonder are found when one stands and observes Mother Earth.

Building Block 10
Strengthen the spirit

> "The most beautiful thing we can experience is the mysterious. Recognition of the mystery of the universe is the source of all true science. He to whom emotions are a stranger, who can no longer pause to wonder and stand rapt in awe is as good as dead; his eyes are closed."
>
> Albert Einstein

We have both emotional and spiritual competencies that help us build resilience. People who have overcome huge adversity will often identify a moment in time when they felt strengthened by something deep within them, rather than just a rational thought. Deep challenge strips away many layers of identity until our core reveals itself. Childhood is meant to be a time when the wonder of seeing the world through children's eyes needs to be valued and appreciated. It has some serious benefits for the developing brain—neural pathways to pleasure rather than pain.

> Childhood is a time of wonder and awe as the world the grabs our attention through our fresh eyes and ears. It is not hard to find a child absorbed in the blissful moment on a swing, or spinning just to feel the world move around them. Children are natural mystics. Sometimes the wonder opens all the way to ecstasy and unity.
>
> *The Secret Spiritual World of Children*, Tobin Hart (2003)

Children need to experience the joy of discovery—feeling rain, jumping into a puddle or a large pile of leaves, touching a kitten, or seeing Christmas tree lights—all for the very first time. The moment of awe must be experienced while young for it to be a powerful part of adult life. These experiences of heightened sensation allow children to feel transcendent—somehow more expanded and larger than life. The search for transcendence can drive later experiences. Those who have had positive natural highs as young children are more likely to seek natural thrills rather than drugs or high risk activities as they become teenagers and adults.

As a culture, Australians are depreciatory in their ability to celebrate. Maybe it's the English 'stiff upper lip' that is still present in many of our genes. We tend to hold back on spontaneous joy as though it is something we need to contain. Our children are also conditioned at an early age to 'settle down' when they are too excited; yet they are in the throes joy or delight. I know that without the laughter and lightness in my home, shared with my boys and their many friends, we would all have experienced more pain and challenges as we journeyed through childhood and the teenage years. Experiences of deep connection can bring forth joy. Music, singing, dancing and awesome moments in nature can result in joy. The simple experiences of being remembered, accepted, validated or thanked all bring forth a bubbling of joy within us—even if we are alone.

At the National Speakers' Conference in Sydney, in March 2003, I was able to experience joy and delight after participating in a drumming session shared with over 150 fellow participants. We were led by two drummers on stage (the Motivational Non-Speakers) and it was quite amazing how they were able to lead totally novice drummers, each with our own drum, to a state of unity and sheer delight—without a word being spoken! Rachael Kessler explains that type of experience as a "wild inventiveness that stirs souls and can release a current of joy "(*The Soul of Education*, 2000).

My sons were very used to being drawn outside when there was a stunning full moon, interesting cloud formations, or cloud bursts as the sun's rays shone through the clouds. And while my boys think their mother is 'missing a few kangaroos in the back paddock', I know they have enjoyed some of the moments too; sometimes they get me to come and watch. I have seen the brilliant sparkle in their eyes when they return from a surfing trip to say that they were joined in the surf by a school of dolphins, or that they saw a whale close by—sheer joy and delight that is provided free of charge by Mother Earth. This connection to nature is starving in many children's lives because of the dominance of the virtual reality world and it must be remedied if we are to heal the serious dislocation of many of today's children and teenagers.

> "Only after the last tree has been cut down;
> Only after the last river has been poisoned;
> Only after the last fish has been caught, will you find that money cannot be eaten."
>
> 19th Century Cree Indian prophecy.

The Health Commission of Western Australia in 2004 found:
- *56 children under 4 were on anti-depressants.*
- *728 children aged 5–9 were on anti-depressants.*
- *4,689 children aged 10–14 were on anti-depressants.*
- *National prescriptions for people under 19 topped more than 250,000 (2004).*
  Another frightening statistic I discovered recently was that Ritalin prescriptions have jumped from 11,500 (1994) to 205,000 (2006).

From my experiences, I would suggest these figures around anti-depressant prescriptions would have doubled in the last four years. The modern culture does not fully support the healthy raising of children. As I write these words on a chilly July day, the global economic climate is appearing quite dismal. While it does not need lots of money to raise healthy children, it does require enough to be able to create safe, nurturing environments with good nutrition, with an absence of deprivation physically, emotionally and spiritually. Some of the happiest children live in third world countries with strong extended family-based communities with simple needs. The busyness of life means that children are being squeezed in between many other things and activities – and often end up feeling invisible or unimportant. Deep profound connection is vital in healthy spiritual and emotional competence and it takes time and energy.

The stronger the human spirit the less disconnected and separated we feel within the world. Just as we have IQ, and EQ I believe we have SQ—Spiritual Quotient.

> Nature is one of our greatest healers. There is healing in the wind, the sun, the moon, the stars, the ocean, the stones, the songs of the birds and the flowers. It is only for us to trust this is so and allow ourselves to receive.
>
> *Hawai'i* by Linda Kaholokai in, *A Little Book of Aloha: Spirit of Healing*, Renata Provenzano (2003).

Spiritual Intelligence

- Wonder.
- Respect and reverence.
- Awe.
- Relational spirituality.
- Lightness and laughter.
- Contemplation.
- Calmness, stillness and quiet.
- Tenderness and gratitude.
- Simplicity.
- Listening with the heart.

Happy children have a strong spirit and know that life is full of anticipation, delight and fun, regardless of adversity. Have you seen the shiny eyes that happy children have especially after diving into a pile of leaves or a big puddle? The more of these experiences children have up to 10 years of age the better. The brain wires all positive experiences like a web over all future experiences and builds a sense of anticipation of how life will be. Children who have had moments of sheer fun and enjoyment will tend to anticipate and expect more of those moments as an adult.

The imaginary world of children is an essential part of strengthening their spirit. Plenty of experiences that include fairy tales, tooth fairies and imaginary friends build a healthy base for a strong spirit and creative mind. These are helpful for building resilient adults.

An absence of a rich imaginary world has been shown to add to the possibility of mental illness and poor motivation when faced with challenge. Modern parents have stopped sharing traditional fairy tales and nursery rhymes because they sometimes have awful things in them. Georgie Porgie made the girls cry, hush a by baby fell out of the tree and Hansel was almost eaten by a witch. Some researchers believe that traditional tales and nursery rhymes were preparing children better for how to be resilient later in life. They showed children that evil existed, that persistence was often needed to overcome adversity and that life hurt at times. Maybe our need to over protect our children is making them softer and less prepared for life as an adult.

> The important thing is to avoid squashing your child's creativity and imagination.
>
> Margot Sunderland.

The following comes from my previous book, *Nurturing Kids' Hearts and Souls*, and clearly shows the value of a healthy imaginative world for children, especially those under 10 years of age.

It was 2001 and a beautiful little five-year-old girl was brought to see me. She was very sad. Her mother told me how the little girl did not play with the other children at pre-school. The doctor wanted to put her on antidepressant medication but her parents were hoping I might be able to help so that they could avoid medication. This little one, who I will call Cindy, began to draw me an intensely black picture, even though I had given her a collection of brightly coloured textas with which to draw. As she drew she asked, "Maggie, how can you die if you want to?" I asked Cindy what she meant. She responded that sometimes when she woke up in the mornings she closed her eyes and tried to die. Her eyes were sad; there was no sparkle or light in them. My heart tugged deeply within me. I explored in my mind where this deep despair could be coming from—both her parents were concerned and loving. What had gone so wrong?

Cindy's parents were professional people. They had decided to give Cindy the 'best opportunity to be successful in life' by promoting the development of her intelligence. Fantasy and the imaginary world were considered to be a distraction to her development. So Cindy had grown up with no tooth fairies, no Father Christmas, no Grimm Brothers fairy tales and certainly no opportunities for imaginary play or dress ups. Unknowingly, these caring parents had starved Cindy's emerging imagination and sucked the life out of her young spirit. They were not aware of the protective role the imagination can play in a young child's life.

Recognising this, we were able to immediately bring wonder and creativity back into Cindy's life. Fortunately, Cindy had a wonderful supportive pre-school teacher who was willing to support us and Cindy wore fairy wings every day for a month. When I saw her next her eyes were shining, she had a beautiful smile and was accompanied by two very happy parents. Cindy is now full of life and energy with her mind, body, and heart and soul all well.

Interestingly, only the week after I first saw Cindy I met another pre-schooler who had a similar story. She too responded quickly to opportunities to play, experience imaginary games and stories and have fun time with her parents. These two little girls came into my office and helped me explore the positive influences that play and imagination have in young people's lives. I am deeply grateful to them for showing me this and the impact a deficit has on healthy mental and physical development. I liken these children to the canaries that were kept in the bottom of the mines in days gone by as a way of alerting the miners to the presence of toxic gases. The girls alerted me to a modern danger for children, and to our future adults, one that can be averted with commonsense rather than medication.

Undoubtedly, for children the gift of the imagination is a powerful source of comfort, distraction and escape. The imagination also helps us all to process life experiences, manage and balance our emotions, enrich our social understandings, explore our spiritual world, develop communication skills and create wonderful possibilities for our lives. It is alright for children to have imaginary play, friends or explanations to help shield them from the often awful, harsh realities of the adult world. Children's imaginations need time and space to develop and a willingness on the part of adults to really honour this gift—not expensive toys. Adulthood comes early enough into our lives and a rich imaginative childhood helps build resilience and coping skills that will last for life. Maybe with more honouring of the imaginative world of children we can turn round the figures of medicated, disconnected children.

A wonderful book that helps build spiritual competence and understanding, especially empathy is, *Grandma's Great Advice* by Julie Ann Harper. If you are seeking books that embrace love, touch the heart, kindle the spirit and enlighten the mind, explore Julie Ann's web site at www.pickawoo.com.

Another way to strengthen the human spirit is with lightness and laughter. Laughter needs to be experienced often so that it becomes an easy part of life. A sense of humour is one of the most important protective factors in terms of resilience, because it helps us reframe a negative experience into a lighter moment. Chemical changes happen in the brain that help us diffuse stress, improve our emotional state and allow us to review the situation from a more optimistic place.(Daniel Goleman,1996, *Emotional Intelligence*). Encourage young children to tell jokes and riddles, and to laugh lots.

The natural world helps strengthen the human spirit whether it is a beautiful garden, a park, mountain or the beach. The open spaces and fresh air automatically release stress and then energise in a healthy and nourishing way. To avoid chaos in the house try taking your family for a walk or to play in the park. A healthy respect and connection to the natural world is a part of all resilient people.

> Spirit is the innermost quality of being. It is that part of us that is unstained, the primordial beauty from which we derive every inspiration, an inborn reservoir from which we can draw every jewel of excellence, the source of universal love and compassion, the clear radiance from which wisdom is born.
>
> Geshe Lobsang Tenzin,Director of the Deprung Monastery in North America, *What is Spirit: Messages from the Heart,* Lexie Brockway Potamkin, (1999).

The human spirit is strengthened by loving relationships where there is genuine positive regard and acceptance. Acts of kindness towards others always builds our own spirit and sense of value. Young children can benefit by becoming involved in simple acts of service and helping others. These opportunities can be very valuable for building emotional and social competence that values our inter-connectedness and our profound need for community. The modern world has seen a serious weakening of social capital and community spirit.

> Human connectedness is the key to resilience, authentic happiness and a sense of well-being. This can only be achieved through the recognition, honouring and nurturing of the human spirit that exists within every child ever born.
>
> *Saving Our Children from Our Chaotic World*, Maggie Dent (2003).

When the family unit is surrounded by a safe circle of love and support, it is a powerful source of comfort and is the most significant thing growing children can experience. No toys, TVs, big houses or expensive schools can replace what happens in such a sacred place as a caring, nurturing family. Communities who protect the families within its boundaries play an enormous role in the healthy raising of children. When a child's needs are at risk, the community must step up and be there for as long as is needed.

It is time to recognise that governments have limited success at a community level because the grass roots reality means that without trust and respect, money is simply money. The synergy that is needed must come from within each community—it is community people with courage and a passionate humanity that hold the light of hope. There is nothing quite like the power of hope and we must never give up on our children.

> "Of all the forces
> That make for a better world
> None is so indispensable
> None so powerful as hope.
> Without hope man is only half alive."
>
> Charles Sawyer (1887-1979)

Children need help to build resilience and self esteem, however they are naturally wired to learn and to realise their potential—whatever that may be. Remember, the little things are sometimes the big things for toddlers and children. We are the guardians and the keepers as the primary carers. We are also companions on the journey, on this interesting thing called life. Whatever we have as our hidden life purpose, may we find the people and opportunities that allow it to unfold through adversity and times of great success. Real kids need slow childhoods that allow them to grow on all levels – mind, body, heart and soul. They need deep connectedness with living things like people and pets to grow in their capacity to build nurturing, loving relationships later in life. This is what we all yearn for and seek and real kids who have been able to be real kids have the best chance at achieving it.

The Prophet

And a woman who held a babe against her bosom said,
    "Speak to us of children." And he said,
    "Your children are not your children. They are the sons
and daughters of Life's longing for itself. They come through
you but not from you. And though they are with you yet they
belong not to you.
    "You may give them your love but not your thoughts, for
they have their own thoughts. You may house their bodies but
not their souls, for their souls dwell in the house of tomorrow
which you cannot visit, not even in your dreams.
    "You may strive to be like them, but seek not to make
them like you. For life goes not backward nor tarries with
yesterday.
    "You are the bows from which your children as living
arrows are sent forth. The archer sees the mark on the path of
the infinite, and he bends you with his might that his arrow may
go swift and far Let your bending in the archer's hand be for
gladness for as he loves the arrow that flies. So he loves the
bow that is stable."

The Prophet, Kahil Gibran (1923)

Parent Tips for Strengthening the Spirit

- *Children need to experience the joy of discovery.*

- *The human spirit is strengthened by loving relationships.*

- *Have special home and classroom rituals that show everyone matters.*

- *Work at building strong caring relationships—no matter how hard it may be.*

- *Feeling loved and valued is essential to a strong spirit.*

- *Allow imagination and wonder to be a part of*

children's lives.

- *Develop a strong connection to the natural world.*

- *Ensure the arts are part of every day—singing, dancing, music, painting, make-believe, story telling.*

- *Laughter and lightness nurture the spirit.*

- *Connection to nature is very important for the growth of the whole child.*

- *Hope is a powerful force—without it there is nothing but profound fear and despair.*

- *Acts of kindness towards others always builds our own spirit and sense of value.*

- *Strengthening communities from the grass roots is essential in building children's resilience and well-being.*

- *Remember the little things are sometimes the big things for toddlers and children.*

- *For children the gift of the imagination is a powerful source of comfort, distraction and escape.*

- *Hope is a unique quality that everyone needs.*

- *A strong spirit will help individuals overcome setbacks and adversity.*

What is Self Esteem?

> Children cannot view themselves directly; they can only know themselves via the feedback and images they receive from significant others. Parents are like mirrors in which children view themselves and these pictures tend to endure into adulthood.
>
> *Parenting with Purpose: Five Keys to Raising Children with Values and Vision*, Reasoner, Robert W., and Lane, Marilyn L. (2007).

At the international Society for Effective and Affective Learning (SEAL) conference in Liverpool in 2005, the man considered as the grandfather of self esteem, Dr Nathaniel Branden, stated that there are more than 100 definitions of self esteem.

Parents frequently express their concerns about their children's self esteem and ask how they can heal a damaged self esteem in their child. It is important to explore what it is, how we can help our children to build a positive self esteem and what to do if a low self esteem is present.

> In my opinion, self esteem is the most important contribution that an adult can make to a child's life. It is the bed rock on which most other personality traits rest and will do more to determine a child's future than any other single factor.
>
> Sky Schultz PhD., in Diane Loomans, *Full Esteem Ahead*.

According to Dr Branden, self esteem has two essential components:

- *Self-efficacy—Confidence in the ability to cope with life's challenges. Self-efficacy leads to a sense of control over one's life.*
- *Self-respect—Experience oneself as deserving of happiness, achievement and love. Self-respect makes possible a sense of community with others.*

The relevance to resilience must now be clear. Self esteem influences our capacity to cope with life's challenges and in some ways it is the immune system of consciousness. A healthy immune system doesn't guarantee you'll never become ill, but it does reduce your susceptibility to illness and can improve your odds for a speedy recovery if you do get sick (Branden).

In its most simplistic form, self esteem is how we perceive ourselves. This is why it can sometimes be hard and frustrating for parents to help when they know their children are struggling. The outward struggle can be sign of a low self esteem, however an aggressive and angry exterior can also suggest a person struggling with low self esteem.

Self-esteem is an intimate experience; it resides in the core of one's being. It is what I think and feel about myself, not what someone else thinks or feels about me. I can be loved by my family, my mate, and my friends, and yet not love myself. I can be admired by my associates and yet regard myself as worthless. I can project an image of assurance and poise that fools almost everyone and yet secretly tremble with a sense of my inadequacy. I can fulfill the expectations of others, and yet fail my own; I can win every honor, and yet feel I have accomplished nothing; I can be adored by millions, and yet wake up each morning with a sickening sense of fraudulence and emptiness.

Healthy Self Esteem, Dr Nathaniel Branden, (1991).
http://www.nathanielbranden.com.

The above quote from Dr Branden's article on self esteem really resonated with me. I appeared to be a very capable student, leader and friend during my final years of high school with many sporting and academic successes. However, it was a mask covering a very desperate low self esteem. When I failed a politics essay in my first semester at university—my first ever essay failure—I walked back to my lodgings and tried to take my own life by swallowing a bottle of pills. Such was the fragile sense of self that I had been hiding. In a way it was a wonderful opportunity for me to learn about how fragile teenagers can be, and that experience allowed me to begin a life long quest on how to build self esteem and resilience in children and teenagers.

For me I had built a belief that I had value because of my academic successes and my intelligence; when that belief shattered with my essay failure I had nothing else to give me any sense of value or worth. The second awareness I discovered, many years later, was that in response to living with a primary carer who struggled with her own low sense of self with distant mothering, I had built a wall of protection around myself that prevented anyone getting close to me. While I may have been everyone's friend and confidante, no one was ever able to witness my vulnerability. This disconnectedness impacted deeply on my suicide attempt. I had no one I could call upon to walk me through my moment of disaster. Connectedness is a key aspect of resilience and something I value enormously in my life today on many levels.

Unfortunately, becoming successful, powerful or well liked does not automatically guarantee good self esteem. In fact, talented and powerful people who doubt their own core value are usually unable to find joy in their achievements no matter how great their external success. This can be seen today by the insatiable drive for some people for more—more work, bigger houses, better cars and striving for that unattainable marker that will bring them peace. What a horrible irony that it lies hidden within us!

Remember, self esteem has to do with what *you* think of you, not what anyone else thinks of you. It's what your child thinks of themselves—not what you think of them. So how does a low self esteem take shape in the minds of our children? I have been exploring this for the last 30 years. I have witnessed students positively change their self esteem over 12 months in my classrooms, and I have worked with thousands of children and teenagers who struggle with the toxic and negative way they view themselves. I trained with Jack Canfield in 1998 in Santa Barbara, and this exposure re-inflamed my passion for understanding how to transform poor self concepts and to build pathways to positive, authentic self esteem. I am proud to be a member of the International Council of Self Esteem—one of only two members from Australia.

The definition of self esteem I am adhering to is:

Self esteem is the ability to choose to experience oneself as competent, to be able to cope with everyday life and particularly life's challenges, and also of being worthy of happiness and goodness (Maggie Dent).

This definition is adapted from Dr Branden's and validates the importance of choice and awareness, as well as the two fold attributes of authentic self esteem of:

- having the basic skills and competencies required to be successful in life; and
- being worthy of happiness and goodness.

Personally, this explained my state of low self esteem at the time of my suicide attempt not only did I choose to feel worthless and undeserving of happiness, respect or goodness, I lacked key resilience protective factors to over come this adverse event in my life.

My studies of neuro linguistic programming (NLP) in the early 1990s has since expanded my understanding of how we create core concepts and beliefs and, more critically, how these beliefs affect the choices we make consciously and unconsciously. It also showed how other influences shape the way we filter every experience we have. Some of these other influences include language, memories, values, attitudes, ethnicity, culture, ancestral influence and meta programs (Diagram, *NLP Model of Communication*). The mind's ability to filter experiences is a key aspect to the choices we make about how we choose to view things. It is much like the example, "Is the glass half full or half empty?"

NLP Model of Communication

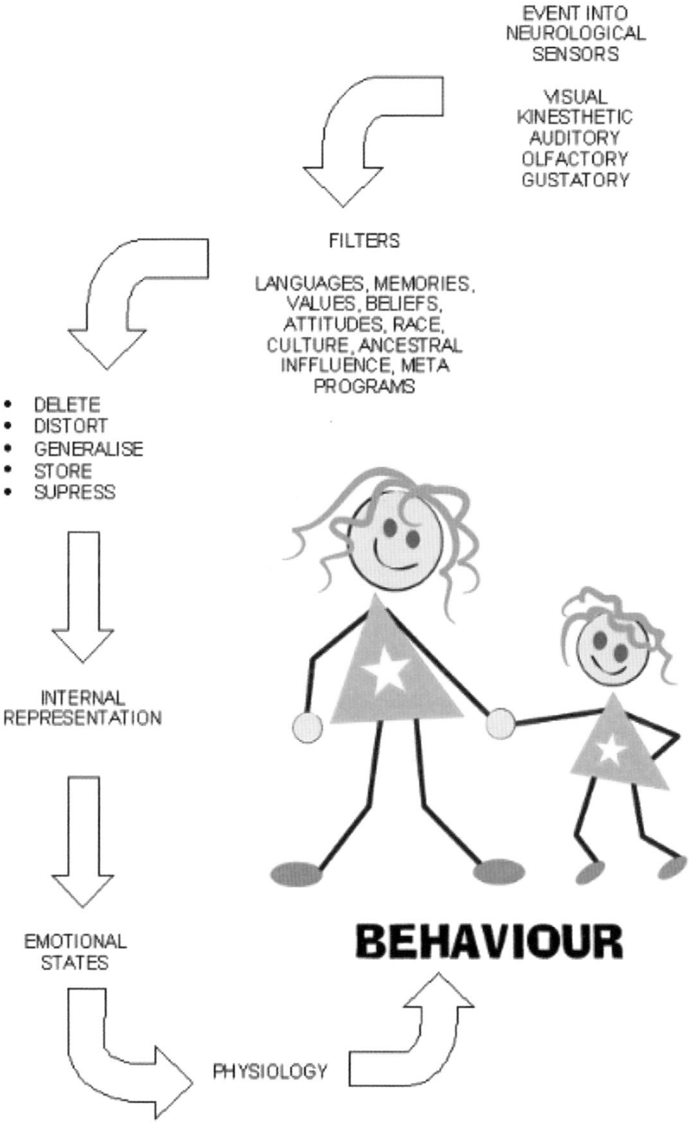

EVENT INTO
NEUROLOGICAL
SENSORS

VISUAL
KINESTHETIC
AUDITORY
OLFACTORY
GUSTATORY

FILTERS

LANGUAGES, MEMORIES,
VALUES, BELIEFS,
ATTITUDES, RACE,
CULTURE, ANCESTRAL
INFFLUENCE, META
PROGRAMS

- DELETE
- DISTORT
- GENERALISE
- STORE
- SUPRESS

INTERNAL
REPRESENTATION

EMOTIONAL
STATES

BEHAVIOUR

PHYSIOLOGY

© Maggie Dent

Cultural differences including language and ancestral patterns can cause significant influences on the emerging self esteem for children. Indigenous children tend to be encouraged to be self-sufficient and develop independence, and can find that the expectations of non-Indigenous teachers who expect children to be pre-trained daunting and challenging (Sharon Spencer, Lecturer, Darwin University, *Every Child Magazine*, Vol 13, No 4, 2007).

Education systems across Australia expect children to arrive with formal learning behaviours and skills pre-learnt. This is a culturally biased style of child rearing and learning that can appear to invalidate Indigenous children at a vital stage of their development. If these children form core concepts that they are in some way wrong or inadequate from this challenge facing them, then this will shape their self esteem for later learning experiences. It is similar in preschools where tactile dominant Indigenous young children who are used to lots of physical touch and affection find that their teachers are unable or unhappy to respond positively to their need for touch. This creates a brain antagonistic environment that will impede their learning, as well as the healthy development of positive core concepts that will shape their self esteem in the future.

Past experiences that are remembered consciously or unconsciously are stored as memories. Children who have been able to play independently in safe environments have a good chance of developing beliefs that will support the development of self-efficacy skills—"I can do for myself"; "I did that all by myself." Future experiences will be filtered via these prior experiences and beliefs. Dr Branden believes that self esteem does not cause behaviour, however it is the container where life's experiences live quietly. There is also a strong tendency for self esteem to generate self-fulfilling prophecies such as, "I feel I am dumb at Maths so I am likely to continue to struggle at maths."

In infancy we learn what is valued, especially by our significant carers, and from this interaction we develop our own invisible value system which shapes who we decide we are. Values are a very significant determiner of behaviour as well. Values are:

- Principles
- Standards
- Morals
- Ethics
- Ideals

Values give us a guiding framework by which to live our lives; they are ideals that guide our behaviour and decisions, and help us distinguish between right and wrong. They also allow us to live in communities with a degree of civility if they are based on positive values, however the reverse can occur as well. These emerging values in children help to shape the choices they make that impact on their behaviour. All of these influence self esteem. The way we are parented shapes our values and beliefs significantly, however there are other influences.

Any emotionally significant experiences—positive or negative—can shape our values and developing beliefs. Being shouted at or shamed in any environment—an educational facility, a neighbour's house or a shopping centre—can reshape your child's core concept system. If it is acceptable to share any of your family's clothes, shoes or belongings without asking, then when you take something from someone outside your family you could be accused of stealing. Can you see how the different values systems can cause confusion to children's developing self esteem?

Shaming, shouting or abuse of any kind damages children's value system because it challenges their beliefs around trust. In my view, these beliefs are the foundations of all other beliefs. Without a secure sense of trust in someone, a place, a faith, a community or in ourselves, we will struggle to develop an authentic, positive self esteem.

> Research has demonstrated that healthy self esteem develops when children feel secure, have a positive sense of self, feel valued by others and feel a sense of competence.
>
> Reasoner, Robert W. et al.

Essentially, infants and children need environments and experiences for the development of healthy self esteems. These experiences in the company of caring adults offer children an opportunity to see themselves mirrored back to them. This is partly what the 10 Resilience Building Blocks model is encouraging in a holistic way. Each building block has values and beliefs embedded into it that support children not only becoming more resilient and capable of managing their lives, they also encourage the growth of authentic  positive self esteem. Healthy self esteem does not occur by accident or as a gift; it has to be cultivated, and nurtured.

> It cannot be attained by being showered with praise, nor by material acquisitions, nor by self-talk, nor by being given unrealistic input. What has been learned in recent years is that one person cannot give another self-esteem.
>
> Reasoner, Robert W. et al.

If we follow the premise that values are driven by concepts or deeply held beliefs that individuals form as a consequence of a life experience that was emotionally significant, or by modelling a significant person, then it must be of concern to everyone. How do we change negative, life negating beliefs or concepts? These negative beliefs will keep creating internal representations (mind videos) that will re-affirm fear based thinking like, "I will fail," "I am no good," and "No one cares."

> "Research has shown there is a 90% correlation between the concepts students hold and their perceived ability to learn within the school system."
>
> Dr Tony Townsend, Professor of Education.

The damage that can be done by a poor concept can impact a child on many levels, mainly unconsciously and without thought.

> An emotionally powerful concept (EPC) is one that creates significant changes in the body, including the brain structures that map the body and influence thinking.
>
> *Learning in the Emotional Rooms: How to create classrooms that are uplifting for the spirit*, J. Joseph (2005).

These EPCs either support learning and are positive, or they create avoidance of the learning opportunity and are negative. Any experience for a child has a potential to be a learning opportunity. Did you have an emotionally numbing experience in childhood that still impacts on your behaviour as an adult? I was asked to leave the school singing group and still struggle singing in public even to this day.

Being laughed at by others when we made a mistake during class or in the playground can influence any similar experience in some way for the rest of your life. Being in a family where a child is chronically hurt or neglected can re-fashion the wiring of the child's brain because of the brain's neuroplasticity. The same goes for a child raised in a secure caring environment; they will be shaped by the social epigenetics that occurs when the child's genes respond to the environment they encounter (Goleman).

Transforming Negative Beliefs

1. Mastery or new powerful positive experiences—including modeling another.
2. Mental rehearsal.
3. Awareness and changing inner-self talk.

The first way to break a negative concept is to achieve mastery or competence in the task. If your child thought they were dumb at maths, a committed teacher who could teach them to do long division or solve a mathematical task would cause structural tension in the belief system. If your child was able to do a few equally successful tasks, the belief can no longer sustain itself and will weaken, and often completely dissolve. The same goes for simple tasks like building blocks, doing puzzles and climbing trees. Every task that succeeds causes tension in the belief system around failure and being useless. The less beliefs that one has that challenge being competent, the more chance a child has of taking more risks with their learning, and also of persevering when success doesn't happen first go.

> Self esteem evolves through the quality of our relationships with each other. It is born within the family because that is where children decide whether they are lovable and capable people. Of course individuals outside the family also influence self esteem. Teachers, coaches and friends all play important roles at different times during our children's growing years.
>
> Caron Goode.

The second way to change negative beliefs is mental rehearsal or the use of creative visualisation. Many children and teenagers have the worst possible vision of themselves; "I am dumb, fat, and useless, no one likes me; I am ugly and no one cares." Some of these children come from very loving families yet the inner critic, or the ego voice, runs an inner dialogue that criticises; it reinforces negative messages we have heard in our childhood. With deep relaxation, particularly with positive visualisation, this critical voice can be quietened so that the unconscious and conscious minds can hear some of the positive messages that reassure young people.

The creation of positive images of themselves can direct children to believe they are capable and acceptable just as they are. Those who perform best have positive mental images that they will achieve well. They often have families that support this by practicing encouragement and evaluative praise, and who focus on the positives in their lives rather than their shortcomings. Now if only we could bring this practice into homes and schools to help those children whose families are unaware of the importance of this in the well-being of their children.

In 1998 I was given a small class of low achievers in English. They were all boys. I decided to work at changing both their mental and emotional perceptions of English classes, and their inner beliefs and perceptions about how well they would perform at the end of term. We created 'The Best Report Ever' visualisation. It involved taking the students into a quiet relaxed place and imagining taking home their very best report ever with comments teachers never write about them, how mum reacts, how dad reacts and how proud they feel within themselves. The students enjoyed the activity as they were able to feel positive about themselves, and the body followed the mind.

What they didn't realise was that their inner perceptions of their potential also changed. No one was more surprised when they started to hand work in—without effort—than the boys themselves. The brain cannot tell the difference between vividly imagined and real experiences, and so after four weeks they began to behave as through they had already taken that great report home. I can proudly say that every one of those boys took home the best report they had ever achieved! They were further surprised because they improved in all their subjects, not just English.

Brain research now shows that new neural connections take time to form—up to 3-4 weeks for it to become unconscious. That is why maximum benefit is gained from children and teenagers who use their mental rehearsal consistently for a month, before trying another one. Reshaping beliefs is like new learning—the more one uses it, the better it will be wired into the neural pathways of the brain.

> The more often an experience repeats, the stronger the habit becomes and the denser the neural connectivity.
>
> Daniel Goleman.

Dr Gerald Jampolsky, Director of the Centre for Attitudinal Learning in the United States created an accelerated learning technique for remedial readers at the elementary level. A group of remedial readers used a tape at home every night for a three month period and at the end of the time they were retested—they had all increased their reading ages, some by as much as four years. The best news was this was achieved without extra tuition or extra work. I have created a visualisation similar to Gerald's on the *School Mastery CD 1* called, *I Can Read Easily*. The teachers using this CD have noticed instant changes in attitude towards reading, and as students moderate all learning through their emotions, this is the first step to changing performance. This is a perfect tool for parents to use at home and is one that the child will enjoy. The final visualisation on this CD is titled, *Accepting Myself*, and it has been successful building self-acceptance in many teenagers and older children.

In NLP, thoughts are believed to direct the language one uses and also influence behaviour. If we can remind students to imagine and say out loud the highest possible outcome or vision for themselves, then we really give them the best opportunity to achieve positive results. We stretch their world of possibilities and for some children, without significant adults who can do that they will struggle to reach their potential. Mental rehearsal works best when linked to a high, emotionally pleasant state. The repetition that is built into visualisations on CDs is very important for building new belief systems in the unconscious mind.

> Parents cannot change every gene, nor modify every neural tic—and yet what children experience day after day sculpts their neural circuitry.
>
> Daniel Goleman.

Real worriers and people with depression have a tendency to frighten themselves with their own negative patterns of thought, especially about the future. They do the 'worst case scenario' and the "What if I fail?", and "I am not good enough," thought patterning and virtually talk themselves into despair and hopelessness. Mental rehearsal has value for everyone because we all have so many levels of consciousness that can be improved.

Creative imagining with the most favourable outcomes is considered an essential activity for fast-tracking personal achievements in all areas of life.

> Self directed imagery and guided stories during which we visualize positive images and hold them in our minds are powerful tools for managing stress and emotional states.
>
> Caron Goode.

I firmly believe that with more awareness of the power of inner thought patterns, visualisation and language—especially for children before 10 years of age—we can help turn around the frightening escalation of failure and low achievement. We can give our children the tools for life that allow them to manage their negative feelings states and their emotionally destructive patterns before they get to puberty when everything accelerates and becomes even more unpredictable. The inclusion of creative visualisations into programs created by psychologists for school children, like in the very successful Friends program, validates the importance of the practice.

The third way to transform negative concepts and their accompanying beliefs is through awareness and consciously changing the inner talk. This is where therapy and counselling has a valid place for children with low self esteem and poor self concepts. With professional help from someone the child values, trusts and respects, significant changes can occur. Caring adults can help a child identify some of their unhelpful patterns, however they sometimes make things worse because children can see that as a form of attack or criticism.

Research shows that reparative therapy can occur when a person shares a painful script from childhood with someone they value and trust and who can provide what their parent was unable to provide. In a way, the therapist can assist the person to rework the original script that may have had quite child-like qualities attached to it. By reworking the experience in an adult framework with a more adult perspective, the person can come to a place of significant healing of the damaged past (Daniel Goleman). There are also many simple techniques that children can learn as games that can dis-empower their negative inner critic. If done as a game they can be really helpful.

There is one other area that demands to be covered in the exploration of self esteem and how to build it in our children. People with an authentic, positive self esteem are usually a delight to be around. They have a delightful sense of fun, play, humour and spontaneity. For this to occur, these people have experienced many moments in childhood that activated intense positive brain chemical and bodily arousal states. This fundamental genetic system for joy must be activated, and how it unfolds depends on the interaction of these genes with social experiences.

This explains to me how I have recovered from the challenging aspects of my childhood with a joyful anticipation of life. Outside of the house I was blessed to be able to run freely around a beautiful farm with 10,000 sheep, interesting bush and incredible freedom to explore the world unencumbered by adult supervision. My siblings and I had to help on the farm and be responsible for taking care of stock, driving farm vehicles and helping whenever needed. There were so many experiences of enormous joy—mulberry fights, endless hours in the local river or farm dams, riding bikes, and wild flower and mushroom picking. There were many bush barbeques and plenty of games of cricket, golf and football. My mum was a great cook who made many excellent meals and morning teas surrounded by family, farm workers and any one who happened to be passing. These repeated happy experiences wired me to appreciate enjoying whatever life brought, and for that I am deeply grateful.

We need to ensure that children have opportunities to experience 'joy juice' for no other reason other than to build a positive foundation for them to maintain or quickly regain a sense of hope, optimism and, 'yes I can' attitude to life.

In this examination of self esteem I must explore the role of praise. A large body of research indicates that children benefit from positive feedback. Yamamoto (1972), for example, provided research that indicated that for every negative criticism a child received, it required a minimum of five positive messages to maintain their self esteem. Many early self esteem strategies therefore emphasised praising children and avoiding negative feedback. Many teachers have relied greatly on gold stars, smiling faces, and decorative stickers to provide positive feedback. Such practices tended blur the distinction between praise and flattery, resulting in a distorted sense of identity. I have worked with girls who have become troubled as teenagers when their parents' praise for their looks diminished. It's easy to call children beautiful, or the best looking girl in the world. It needs to be done with caution now that we can see how these beliefs can be formed where the girls think that is the main reason you love or notice them. The same goes for bright students as research has shown this can be a limiting influence when they get older. If they have been praised because they were smart, they sometimes stop taking learning risks because they fear not being smart enough.

Some children develop unrealistic impressions of what they can do, believing all the praise they receive, much of it not related to specifics. Other children become what might be termed 'praise junkies', striving only for adulation from others. In the absence of such praise they cease to be motivated and can become quite angry at being treated less than special. It is better to encourage effort because it gives children a variable they can control, whereas their intelligence or their looks are ones they cannot control, and this can create stumbling blocks to their perception of their self.

In some early years classes teachers are asked to avoid saying "No," to young children in some misguided notion it can damage the young child's self esteem. This is ridiculous in terms of building resilience and healthy self esteem. Having sanctions and boundaries helps children know how to navigate the big, wide world. Adults are responsible to help children learn strategies to deal with failure, success and disappointment. Genuine realistic encouragement is so much better than praise, even if that sometimes means jumping up and down with glee when our son or daughter finishes fifth in the 100 meters sprint. Coming first could be met with the same delight—it's the act of participating and finishing that we need to keep celebrating.

The level of self esteem in children can be enhanced when significant adults and peers treat them with respect, and when there are strong feelings of trust. This trust will allow their views, preferences, and opinions to be considered; and where they have opportunities to make real decisions and choices about events and things that matter to them. Parents who remind children that they make choices all the time—even when they don't choose they are making a choice—are helping their children build reflective, flexible thinking strategies that will help them through life. Life is simply a journey of choices and no matter what happens everyone buggers up at some stage. Perfection is not encouraged, however excellence can be achieved with due effort and diligence. If parents aim to build character rather than academic or physical excellence I believe children would benefit enormously.

> Character is shaped by life experience and cannot be seen from the outside or from physical appearances. It cannot be judged by prizes and accolades. Nor can it be judged by age or culture. Character can only be ascertained from how a person lives and interacts with others.
>
> *Nurturing Kids' Hearts and Souls*, Maggie Dent (2005).

Character education is an intentional effort to identify and foster positive virtues and values in children so they can make choices that reflect caring, respect, personal responsibility, honesty and integrity. This is an excellent way to support the growth of authentic self esteem in our children. It would help counteract the shallow, consumer driven modern world of 'instant' and 'must have'. To build character would help children appreciate that the pursuit for the greater good will also allow for personal greatness. This would hopefully enable our world to become a more caring, compassionate and better place to be.

The core belief I encourage children to value is that every child ever born is born with gifts and talents that are unique to them and they can use these gifts positively to somehow make the world a better place.

One of my toughest lessons as a mum was to stop running lunches to school when my boys forgot them. Tough love is tough for both parties, and yet it is an effective way to allow our children to grow both emotionally and socially, and to accept responsibility for their own actions and choices. This will give them self-efficacy, or a confidence in being able to cope with life's challenges. This ability will give them a sense of control over one's life. Nathaniel Brandon author of, *The Seven Pillars of Self Esteem* believes this has to be a key quality for authentic self esteem. Children can only learn this by having the opportunity to make choices and have input into the experiences that occur. How often do we get children to put jackets on because it is cold and yet the child is actually quite warm because they have been running around? The 'just in case' reasoning of parents can invalidate a child's emerging decision making. We need to let them practise and see the consequences of their choices and actions. Let them work out what cold and wet is by experiencing it for themselves.

Each of the 10 resilience building blocks gives opportunities to build the six pillars of self esteem that Dr Branden believes builds authentic self esteem.

1. *Living consciously—Paying attention to information and feedback about needs and goals; facing facts that might be uncomfortable or threatening; refusing to wander through life in a self-induced mental fog.*

2. *Self-acceptance—Being willing to experience whatever we truly think, feel or do, even if we don't always like it; facing our mistakes and learning from them.*

3. *Self-responsibility—Establishing a sense of control over our lives by realising we are responsible for our choices and actions at every level; the achievement of our goals, our happiness and our values.*

4. *Self-assertiveness—The willingness to express appropriately our thoughts, values and feelings; to stand up for ourselves, to speak and act from our deepest convictions.*

5. *Living purposefully—Setting goals and working to achieve them, rather than living at the mercy of chance and outside forces and developing self-discipline.*

6. *Integrity—The integration of our behavior with our ideals, convictions, standards and beliefs and acting in congruence with what we believe is right.*

Six Pillars of Self-Esteem, Dr. N. Branden (1994).

Each of the 10 resilience building blocks have the potential to embed helpful beliefs and values into children's developing brains that can enhance a healthy self esteem.

1.   Positive healthy pregnancy
- I am wanted.
- My world is safe.
- I matter.

2.   **Good nutrition**
- I am cared for.
- I am nurtured.
- Good food makes me feel good.

3.   **Safe nurturing care**
- I am loved.
- I am valued.
- People value me.
- I can get my needs met.

4.   **Plenty of play**
- Life is fun.
- I can make choices.
- I can share and take turns.

5.   **Life skills**
- I can learn new things.
- I can become smarter anytime.
- It's OK to make mistakes.

6.   **Meaningful involvement**
- I matter.
- I am noticed.
- People care.
- I am loved.

7.   **Clear boundaries**
- I am safe.
- Routine calms my world.
- I am a child and this is OK.
- Boundaries protect me.

8.   Absence of stress
- I can be quiet and still.
- Calmness feels good.
- I can take my time.
- Sleep is good for me.

9.   Self mastery
- I am capable.
- With practise I improve.
- Success feels good.
- Real experience is my best teacher.

10.   Strengthen the spirit
- I can be happy.
- Life can be full of awe and wonder.
- Laughter makes me feel good.
- My imagination is valuable.
- Kindness matters.

These hidden values and their accompanying beliefs can be formed within the context of each of the building blocks. They will support the growth of a healthy self esteem.

> Nurturing kids' hearts and souls is the most effective way of helping build a healthy self esteem and self concept, and this begins early in life.
>
> Maggie Dent

Over my years of teaching, counselling and consultation with families I have noticed that children who know they are loved and accepted unconditionally, have the most authentic, healthy self esteem. This may seem totally obvious, however just because a parent loves their child does not necessarily mean the child knows or feels that love. The loving connection that children feel does not come from having a tidy bedroom, or every new toy or gadget, or from the food we cook for them; it comes from being accepted and embraced for being unique, and different. It is there when children do well and behave quietly, and it must still be there when they struggle with their world and challenge us.

How to Ensure that Your Child Feels Loved?

Firstly, remember that every child is unique and different; what works for one child may not work for another. Secondly, the metaphor of a 'love cup' is really helpful to remember. If your child's love cup is full they feel loved; if not, they may feel disconnected, unloved and un-special. Children often tell me they just feel "Yucky!' Hug them tenderly, look into their eyes when they speak with you, and be kind more often than trying to be right. Unfortunately, I cannot remember being held tenderly by my mother when I was young. I am a highly kinaesthetic person so this was a serious deprivation in my life. If I had been more dependent on vision or sound as my first sense it may have been less of a problem for me. Physical touch and intimacy is really important for my well-being and I am blessed to be surrounded by an abundance of it in my life now.

An excellent book that explains how to fill your child's love cup is, *The Five Love Languages of Children* by Gary Chapman and Ross Campbell. There are five ways that we fill our children's love cup.

1.   *Physical touch—Children and teenagers who really love physical touch will often touch you, sometimes in an annoying way. This is why some boys love to fight or wrestle with their Dad; it is an intimate safe touch that fills their love cup. No electronic screen can give a child positive touch.*
2.   *Words of affirmation—Hearing words of love, encouragement, guidance and appreciation works for*

some children. They are sensitive to tone and criticism and need to often hear, "I love you".

3.   *Quality time—If this is the primary way your child feels loved, then they may sometimes drive you nuts with wanting your full attention. They value real eye contact, one-on-one time, real conversations, sharing feelings and bedtime rituals.*

4.   *Gifts—These children are very attached to the gifts you have bought them over the years and rather than be concerned with cost, size or shape, they are more tuned into the thought you put into purchasing the gift. Be very careful about buying meaningful gifts and of bribery and manipulation as your child will know the difference.*

5.   *Acts of service—These children respond to acts of service, and notice and mention when you cook their favourite meal, come to watch them play sport or make their school lunch in good time. The main motivation must be love, not manipulation or to get something. Also be mindful of making requests and not commands.*

I recommend that you read *The Five Love Languages of Children* and explore with your child their preferred love language; see how you can build on their feelings of being loved. The more unconditionally loved a child feels, the better their self esteem and the healthier their sense of self. It can be anyone in their safe circle of family – not necessarily a biological family member, although it is of course preferable.

Babies form emotional memories and beliefs from pre-birth. This means parents have a huge responsibility to become aware of and knowledgeable about what impacts on our children's emotional, social and spiritual competences. Resilience and self esteem can be nurtured through quality care from primary care givers—mainly family. If they work on strengthening each of the resilience building blocks as their child grows—understanding that perfection is never the aim in the healthy raising of children—they are working towards solutions for many of the challenges that the modern world has created. Real kids need to experience as many of the building blocks as possible as they grow from being a baby to a toddler to a child.

> The best way to inspire your children to develop into the kind of adults you dream of them becoming is to become the kind of adult you want them to be.
>
> Robin Sharma

Keeping the Dream Alive

We tried so hard to make things better for our kids that we made them worse.

For my grandchildren, I'd know better.

I'd really like for them to know about hand-me-down clothes and home-made ice cream and leftover meatloaf. I really would.

My cherished grandson, I hope you learn humility by surviving failure and that you learn to be honest even when no one is looking.

I hope you learn to make your bed and mow the lawn and wash the car— and I hope nobody gives you a brand new car when you are sixteen.

It will be good if at least one time you can see a baby calf born, and you have a good friend to be with you if you ever have to put your old dog to sleep.

I hope you get a black eye fighting for something you believe in.

I hope you have to share a bedroom with your younger brother. And it is all right to draw a line down the middle of the room, but when he wants to crawl under the covers with you because he's scared, I hope you'll let him.

And when you want to see a Disney movie and your little brother wants to tag along, I hope you take him.

I hope you have to walk uphill with your friends and that you live in a town where you can do it safely.

If you want a slingshot, I hope your father teaches you how to make one instead of buying one. I hope you learn to dig in the dirt and read books, and when you learn to use computers, you also learn how to add and subtract in your head.

I hope you get teased by friends when you have your first crush on a girl, and that when you talk back to your mother you learn what Ivory soap tastes like.

May you skin your knee climbing a mountain, burn your hand on the stove and stick your tongue on a frozen flagpole.

I hope you get sick when someone blows smoke in your face. I don't care if you try beer once, but I hope you won't like it. And if a friend offers you a joint or any drugs, I hope you are smart enough to realise that person is not your friend.

I sure hope you make time to sit on a porch with your granddad or go fishing with your uncle.

I hope your mother punishes you when you throw a baseball through a neighbour's window; and that she hugs you and kisses you when you give her a plaster of Paris mould of your hand.

These things I wish for you— tough times and disappointment, hard work and happiness.

Lee Pitts, Internet.

Recommended Texts

Aldort, Naomi, (2005), *Raising Our Children, Raising Ourselves: Transforming Parent-child relationships from reaction and struggle to freedom, power and joy*, Book Publishers Network, USA.

Bernard,B., (1991), *Fostering Resiliency in Kids: Protective Factors in the Family School and Community*, Portland, OR. North West Education Library.

Branden, Nathaniel, *Healthy Self Esteem*, [internet] http://www.nathanielbranden.com

Brooks, R. and Goldstein, S., (2001), *Raising Resilient Children*, McGraw Hill, USA.

Brooks, R. and Goldstein, S., (2003), *Nurturing Resilience in Our Children : Answers to the Most Important Parenting Questions*, McGraw Hill, USA.

Cecich, Leonie, (2005 and 2006), *You Gotta Get Up*, Kids'n'Music Publication, Perth, WA.

Canfield, J. and Siccone, F., (1995), *101 Ways to Develop Self -Esteem and Responsibility*, Simon and Schuster, Mass. USA.

Chapman, Gary & Campbell, Ross (2002*) The Five Love Languages of Children."*Strand Publishing, Sydney.

Clouder, Christopher and Nicol, Janni, (2007), *Creative Play for Your Baby: Steiner Waldorf expertise and toy projects for 3 months-2 years*. Octopus Publishing, London.

Cunningham, H., (2006), *The Invention of Childhood*, BBC Books, London.

Deakin, J.,(2006), *Dangerous People, Dangerous People: the nature and location of young people's victimisation and fear in children, in Children and Society*.

Dent, Maggie, (2003), *Saving Our Children from Our Chaotic World: Teaching Children the Magic of Silence and Stillness*, Pennington Publications.

Dent, Maggie, (2005), *Nurturing Kids' Hearts and Souls: Building Emotional, Social and Spiritual Competence*, Pennington Publications.

Dingle, Dr. Peter, (2004), *The Deal for Happier, Healthier Smarter Kids: A Twenty First Century Survival Guide for Parents.*

Dingle, Dr. Peter (2008) My Dog Eats Better then your Kids: Perth WA

Fox, Mem and Argent, Kerry, (1995), *Wombat Divine*, Gosford, Aust, Omnibus Books.

Garner, H., (1993), *Multiple Intelligences: The Theory In Practice*, New York, Basic Books.

Garth, Maureen, (1993), *Starbright, Moonbeam, Earthlight: Meditations for Children*, Harper Collins Publishers, Australia.

Gibran, Kahil, (1926), *The Prophet,* Mandarin Paperback, London.

Gill, Tim, (2007), *No Fear :Growing Up in a Risk Averse Society*, Calouste Gulbenkian Foundation, London.

Goleman, D., (1996), *Emotional Intelligence: Why it Can Matter More Than IQ*, UK, Bloomsbury Publishing.

Goleman D ,(2006) *Social Intelligence: The New Science of Relationships, Random House, London,*

Goode, Caron B., (2001), *Nurture Your Child's Gift: Inspired Parenting*, Beyond Words Publishing, Oregon, USA.

Gonzalez-Mena, Janet and Widmeyer Eyer, Dianne, (2004), *Infants, toddlers and caregivers: The Philosophy of Respect based on the work by Magda Gerber and the Hungarian paediatrician Emmi Pikler*, Mc Graw Hill, New York.

Grille, R., (2005), *Parenting for a Peaceful World*, Longueville Media.

Grille, R., (2008), *Heart to Heart Parenting, Nurturing your child's emotional intelligence from conception to school age,* ABC Books, Australia.

Hamilton, Maggie (2008) What's Happening to Our Girls: Too much, Too Soon, How Our Kids are Oversold, Overstimulated and Oversexed. Penguin Books , Aust.

Harper, Julie Ann and Rose, Maree Rose, *Grandma's Great Advice,* Pick-a-woo Publishers, Western Australia.

Jensen, Eric, (2006), *Enriching the Brain*, Jossey-Bass.USA

Koutsoukis, David (2005) 366 Fun Facts you Never Needed to Know, Funstar Publishing, Perth, WA

Koutsoukis, David (2005) 3666 Fun Quotes and Observations on Life, Funstar Publishing, Perth, WA.

Loomans, Diane, (1994), *Full Esteem Ahead: 100 Ways to Build Self Esteem in Children and Adults.*

Lipsett, Rhodanthe (2007) Second Edition, *No 'One Right Way'* Publisher - Sea Change Publishing , Kingscliff, Aust.

Mann, Anne, (2005), *Motherhood: How should we care for our children*, Allen & Unwin. Australia.

McGrath, Helen and Noble, Toni, *Bounce Back Teacher's Handbook: Bounce Back: A Classroom Resilience Program*, Pearson Education, NSW.

McLachlan, L., and Kummer C.,(2004), *Kindayoga*, Wild Journey Films, Sydney, NSW.

Medved, Michael and Medved, Diane, PhD, (1999*), Saving Childhood: Protecting Our Children from the National Assault on Innocence,* Harper Collins Publishers, USA.

Mosley, J., and Sonnet, H., *Wet Playtime Games, Clapping Games (with CD), More Clapping Games (with CD), Skipping Games , Playground Games, Singing Games (with CD) music by Caroline Radcliffe.*

Moorman, Chick and Haller, Thomas, (2005), *The 10 Commitments: Parenting with Purpose*, Personal Power Press, USA.

Neumann, Michelle M., (2007), *Up Down: A Fun and Practical Way to Introduce Reading and Writing to Children aged 2-5*, Finch Publishing, Lane Cove, Australia.

Pearce, Joseph Chilton, (2002), *The Biology of Transcendence: A Blueprint of the Human Spirit*, Park Stuart Press.USA

Peterson C., Maier, S.F. and Seligman M.E.P., (1995), *Learned Helplessness: A Theory for the Age of Personal Control*, Hoeber.

Porter, Dr. Louise, (1994), *Children are People Too: A parents' guide to young children's behaviour*, South Australia, East Street Publications.

Reasoner, Robert W. and Lane, Marilyn L., (2007), *Parenting with Purpose: Five Keys to Raising Children with Values and Vision*, Personhood Press, USA.

Reivich, K. and Shatte, A., (2002), *The Resilience Factor*, Broadway Books.

Rush, Emma and La Nauze, Andrea, (2006), *Letting Children be Children: Stopping the sexualisation of children in Australia*, The Australia Institute: ACT, TAI Discussion Paper 93, December 2006.

Stanley, Prof. Fiona, Richardson, Sue and Prior, Margot, (2005), *Children of the Lucky Country : How Australian society has turned its back on its children and why children matter*, Pan McMillan.

Starr, Raymond, (1998), quoted in Diamond, M and
Hopson, J., *Magic Trees of the Mind: How to
Nurture Your Child's Intelligence, Creativity and
Healthy Emotions from Birth through
Adolescence,* Dutton, New York.

Sunderland, Margot, (2007), *The Science of
Parenting: How Today's Brain Research can
Help you Raise Happy, Emotionally Balanced
Children*, DK Publishing, New York.

Hart, Tobin PhD., (2003), *The Secret Spiritual World
of Children*, Inner Ocean Publishing, Hawai'i,
USA.

Wagele, Elizabeth, (2007), *Finding the Birthday
Cake: Helping Children Raise their Self Esteem*,
New Horizon Press, NJ, USA.

Walker, Kathy, (2005*), What's The Hurry: Reclaiming
Childhood in an Overscheduled World*, ASG,
Australia.

Weise, Jo and Wells, Steve, (2004), *Rose and The
Night Monsters*, Inglewood, Western Australia,
Waterford Press, [internet] www.eftdownunder.com.